Women and Work
Inequality in the Canadian Labour Market
Revised Edition

Paul Phillips and Erin Phillips

James Lorimer & Company, Publishers
Toronto, 1993

James Lorimer and Company Ltd. acknowledges with thanks the support of the Canada Council, the Ontario Arts Council and the Ontario Publishing Centre in the development of writing and publishing in Canada.

Cover photo: Paul Venning/Masterfile

Canadian Cataloguing in Publication Data

Phillips, Paul, 1938-
  Women and work: inequality in the Canadian
labour market

Rev. ed.
Includes bibliographical references.
ISBN 1-55028-426-6 (bound) ISBN 1-55028-427-4 (pbk.)

1. Women - Employment - Canada. I. Phillips,
Erin, 1961 -   . II. Title.

HD6099.P48 1993   331.4'0971   C93-093808-9

James Lorimer & Company, Publishers
Egerton Ryerson Memorial Building
35 Britain Street
Toronto, Ontario
M5A 1R7

Printed in Canada

For Lauren and Molly

Contents

Introduction to the Second Edition

It is now over two decades since the Royal Commission on the Status of Women documented the economically inferior position of women in contemporary Canadian society. The Commission's report confirmed what many women had been complaining about for some time — that women's incomes were lower and their employment opportunities more circumscribed. But it also showed that women faced other, less obvious, barriers to economic equality, such things as limited access to higher occupational levels and to management positions, difficulty in getting credit, and inadequate old age security. The work of the Commission gave impetus to women's organizations, governments, unions and other bodies to initiate programs and policies designed to reduce these disparities in economic opportunities and to alter the social attitudes and institutions that gave rise to economic discrimination against women.

The first edition of our book, *Women and Work,* was an attempt to evaluate the progress that had been made in the decade or so after the Commission's report was first issued. Our report card, mirroring the Commission's own ten year assessment, indicated our disappointment. What we wrote at the time bears repeating.

During the seventies, little significant progress was made towards reducing wage and employment disparities between men and women or in changing discriminatory social attitudes and institutions. The economic disadvantage women face in the market for labour has been documented since biblical times and was actually embodied in medieval British law as early as the Statute of Labourers in 1383. Over the last century in Canada, women's average incomes remained relatively constant at approximately 60 per cent of men's while women's range of occupational opportunities actually narrowed slightly by 1980 when 80 per cent were confined to four occupational groups: professional (mainly nursing and teaching); clerical; commercial and financial; and service. This constancy of labour market disadvantage occurred despite a massive movement of women into the work-force since the 1960s.

Nor was there much evidence of progressive social change despite some significant legislative breakthroughs in women's legal rights. These laws (family law reform, pay and employment equity measures and maternity leave provisions) were largely contradicted by repeated demonstrations that Canadians and Americans, politicians and the general public alike, did not take sexual equality seriously.

Now, a second decade has passed. Can we be more optimistic that progress is being made in eliminating the labour market discrimination women have traditionally faced? Is there any more evidence that attitudes and institutions have altered in favour of gender equality? Perhaps the most we can say is that there are some indications of progress. The ratio of average earnings (rather than income referred to previously) of full-year, full-time women workers relative to men workers has risen fairly steadily, though slowly, since the late 1970s. In 1976 women's earnings as a percentage of men's earnings stood at 60.2 per cent. In 1990 the comparable figure was 67.6 per cent. The *Ontario Green Paper On Pay Equity* of 1985 estimated that wage discrimination within the same narrowly defined job classifications accounted for only a little over 10 per cent of this earnings differential. At the same time five provinces have adopted proactive pay equity statutes (equal pay for work of equal value) though only Ontario's extends beyond the public sector.

The evidence on occupational distribution, on the other hand, shows little evidence of any marked improvement in women's access to non-traditional jobs. It is true that the percentage of women in managerial and administrative occupations has risen quite markedly (though much of the increase has been concentrated in the lower and subordinate ranks). However, according to the 1986 census, three quarters of all women were employed in the teaching and health occupations, or were clerical, sales or service workers. A further 8 per cent were in the managerial and administrative category. A remarkable 60 per cent were nurses or teachers, clerical workers, sales clerks or food and beverage service workers (waitresses, barmaids, cooks). Among the major manufacturing occupations, almost 40 per cent of all women were garment or textile workers. Inequity in access to jobs (which the Ontario pay equity study estimates accounts for two to three times the inequality in average earnings that is caused by wage discrimination) has proven the more intractable problem, despite the more proactive employment equity stance of the federal government and the Canadian Human Rights Commission.

What is more encouraging is the progress of women in the labour movement. Across the country, women have been assuming more and more of the top executive positions. Perhaps a good example of this is that until the recent retirement of Shirley Carr as president of the Canadian Labour Congress, the presidents of the CLC, the Manitoba Federation of Labour and the Winnipeg Labour Council were all women. As well, the percentage of organized labour that is female has been rising and unions have become increasingly attentive to what can generally be referred to as "women's issues" in negotiations.

Despite these positive indications, however, there have been a number of ominous developments. One has been termed the "feminization of poverty." According to the 1990 study by Gunderson, Muszynski and Keck for the Canadian Advisory Council on the Status of Women, *Women and Labour Market Poverty*, the proportion of poor who were women rose from just under 46 per cent in 1971 to almost 60 per cent by 1986. Women were over a third more likely to be in poverty than were men.

The second negative portent for female equality was the emergence of the neo-conservative economic agenda in the 1980s — free trade, restructuring, deregulation, privatization, retrenchment in the public sector and in social programs, and the assault on unionism. We will document the negative impact of these developments on the economic prospects for women in later chapters. It is clear that the unregulated labour market does a very poor job in ensuring equality of either economic opportunities or income results. Therefore, the movement to more and more unrestricted labour markets is a recipe for increased inequality, with obvious negative prospects for women and other disadvantaged groups in the labour market.

Before we can attempt to understand this new challenge to women's economic equality in the labour market, however, we must understand the nature, extent and causes of labour market discrimination. Is it rooted in overt male discrimination against women or in the failure of women to acquire the skills and behaviour patterns that are valued in the marketplace? Is it biological differences between the sexes that restrict female participation in work or is it social organization, attitudes and institutions that, wittingly or unwittingly, discriminate against women? These are questions we will pursue in this book, first through an historical review of women's work in Canada, and secondly through an in-depth look at the nature of the contemporary market situation of women workers. With this background, we can explore the challenges and prospects for the future.

What are those challenges? The most obvious and immediate is the technological, structural and geographic restructuring that has been underway for the last decade, encouraged by the neo-conservative policy agenda referred to above. Its impact will be felt on traditional male work as well as on women's. The way men respond can have either positive or negative implications for women's prospects. Will men try to protect themselves at the expense of women? Or will men realize that both sexes are victims of the same processes and adopt a common and complementary program?

A great deal will depend on the strength and unity of the labour movement and on women's participation in it. Unions have been important in improving the status of workers, not just in terms of monetary compensation but also in job security, career opportunities, and numerous fringe benefits. Worker participation in decision making in what is arguably the most important aspect of daily life, work, has also increased through union efforts. As noted, women's participation in unions has been increasing but it is still lower than men's. As well, unionism overall has been under attack and is in decline, particularly in the private, goods-producing sector. We must explore the implications of these trends for women.

Some reviewers of the earlier edition of this book were critical of the fact that, in their view, we did not pay sufficient attention to women's unpaid work in the home. We did try to explain that though we did not discuss women's double work load (work in the home as well as in the marketplace), it was the starting point of our whole analysis. We argued that women's labour market participation, wage and occupational structure, and lack of career opportunities were directly related to their primary responsibility for work in the home. However, we concentrated in the text on paid work, on the effects of the "double ghetto" on women in the labour market and, consequently, on how their economic status has been incorporated into the prevailing economic structure.

Perhaps we should elaborate a little more on the importance of home work in shaping women's lives in and out of the labour market. To do justice to the topic and the burgeoning literature on it, however, would require more time and space than we have available. Therefore we have included in our "Notes on Sources and Further Reading" references to some of the works, particularly Canadian ones, related to the topics, but we do not intend to survey this material here.

Rather, we will very briefly state what we see as the connection between home work and labour market work with the expectation that readers will keep this in mind as they progress through the following chapters.

First, we should note that non-paid work in the home is of very great importance to the real income of Canadians. Estimates vary, but on average come to the conclusion that home work probably accounts for around 40 per cent of the value of total market incomes. That is, almost a third of all our real standard of living originates in unpaid work in the home, most of it — three quarters or more — contributed by women.

Biology dictates that only women can reproduce. Biology, however, does not dictate all of the social and economic relations that follow. For most of human history, when the household was the primary institution of production and distribution, a sexual division of labour prevailed based on the most efficient allocation of tasks within the family unit as well as the necessity for women to nurture infants. At the simplest level women concentrated on nurturing and home-based tasks, men on external tasks and those involving physical strength. Still, most work, in and out of the home, involved a considerable amount of drudgery.

With the expanding role of the market relating primarily to external work, "men's" work became increasingly valued in the marketplace while "women's" home work became increasingly un-valued and, in consequence, undervalued. Some traditional women's work was incorporated into the market — particularly clothing and textile manufacture, pottery making, food preparation and related household work — drawing women into paid factory work, particularly in the nineteenth century, and thereby intensifying the growing double work burden on women. The undervaluing of home work, however, also led to an undervaluing of market work, and since men's work was the major form of market work and better paid, men became the "primary" wage earners, further degrading women's paid work.

As male real wages increased in the latter decades of the nineteenth century, it became possible for middle-class women to withdraw from market work and reduce the double burden. Ideologically this was incorporated in the "cult of domesticity" which glorified women's unpaid home work while deprecating paid work. Working-class women were not so fortunate. Though forced by biology, ideology and patriarchal power to shoulder the major burden of home work, they were also forced by economic need to conduct some form of money income generating activity, whether it be home work (sewing, washing, baking), growing vegetables, taking in boarders, or more rarely, taking paid employment.

Rising real family incomes in the twentieth century allowed a higher proportion of women to reduce the double work load, though at a significant cost — complete income dependency on their partners. However, from the 1960s on, women began moving back into the labour market in an unprecedented way. Whatever the reasons for this (and they will be explored in Chapter 3), the result was an intensification of the double burden, made much more onerous by the systematic undervaluation and low esteem of household work.

Thus, the relationship between home and market work is a continuing and dynamic one which can not be ignored in devising programs and policies (discussed in Chapters 5, 6, and 7) to promote gender equity in the labour market. One obvious method of reducing the double burden on women is for men to take on more family responsibilities. However, given that men are normally paid more and have more career opportunities, it is usually not economically rational for them to do so if it impinges upon their market work. These are some of the issues we intend to pursue here.

We have attempted throughout to use inclusive language rather than the sexist language so deeply imbedded in our industrial culture. One of the encouraging developments has been the trend toward gender neutral usage in labour studies, perhaps the best example being the replacement of "fishermen" with "fishers" common now to most maritime studies. In the odd place, however, we have consciously retained conventional forms — "craftsman" and "foreman," for example — as a reflection of reality, a reminder that, at least until recently, these were sexually determined positions. One should read this as historical reality, however, not as contemporary or future designation, though both these terms still dominate in collective agreements and legislation.

We have intentionally not tried to fit our analysis into any single school of thought regarding women in the economy. Rather we have tried to draw on insights from research that has been done from many perspectives — orthodox, institutional, feminist and radical. What we have attempted to develop is our own analysis that incorporates elements of all schools and that is a realistic interpretation of the world as it is.

It is impossible to list all of the people who have aided us in this project, both in the preparation of the first and now the second edition. To attempt to select a few would be to slight the contribution of others, so we will not do so. But we would like to dedicate it to someone whom we hope will have more equitable opportunities in her future, perhaps in part because of this book; and to her great grandmother who continues to do her part in the struggle for social justice and equality.

1

Women's Work in Canada:
The Historical Perspective

History and Herstory

Women have not been treated well by history or, at least until recently, by historians. The more we learn of the past, the greater our awareness that women have been forced to play an unequal role in the economy. There is a causal connection between such factors as women's role in reproduction, their assignment to do unpaid work in the home, the social institutions and attitudes of a patriarchal society, the imperatives of industrial capitalism, and the inhumanity of unregulated markets, and the pervasive and persistent inferior economic status of women.

It is fashionable these days to refer to the "working woman" as if this were a recent phenomenon. But what is new about women working? Women have always worked, in many times and places many more hours than men. The difference in recent years is that women are increasingly part of the paid labour force, receiving money incomes for their efforts. Of course, some women have always taken part in the labour market, but they were a small, and usually transitory, minority. It is only since the Second World War that this has changed. It is in the evolution of women's work from the home to the market that we can look for some understanding of the roots of the structure of economic reward in our era.

The Pre-Industrial Period

Wage labour has been a relatively new experience for most Canadian workers of both sexes. The wage labour market only developed between 100 and 150 years ago, and only well into this century did the majority of working people actually work for wages. For most of human history the vast majority of people toiled in a non-wage economy. The common economic unit of production was the family, to which all members, except the youngest of children, contributed.

Canada's fur traders found out early that women were indispensable. The North West Company men took native wives immediately, and when the Hudson's Bay Company tried to forbid their men from following this practice, it had to recant in order that it might be competitive. The skills of the native women, learned in their own culture, were essential for survival. They made moccasins, snowshoes and pemmican, gathered the gum necessary to make the birch-bark canoes, and treated hides. In commerce they acted as interpreters for the traders, and marriage to a native woman brought with it the protection of her tribe. These attributes, so necessary to the nomadic economy of the fur trade, were not required for the settled life of the farmer. As the area which is now called Canada became settled, and agriculture, forestry and other economic pursuits replaced the fur trade, the native women gave way to women from Europe.

The family remained the primary unit of production until this form of work organization was destroyed by industrialization and the factory. There was, of course, a sexual division of labour within the family, a division which appears to have remained more or less unaltered since people first settled on the land. Women would work mainly around the home where they could watch over the children. But they would also do work that was traditionally considered "men's work" in addition to their own when need dictated. In today's world it is easy to overlook the importance of children in this early economy. The bearing and raising of children was central to the survival of the family, as children soon became an economic asset contributing to family production.

Women's work around the home was crucial to family income. Housework kept the family in clothing and food. Particularly in the settlement period when farm families were toiling to fill the requirements of gaining title to land grants, every bit of cash income was needed for capital, machinery and stock. In addition to their responsibilities for the house, children and health care, women worked the farmyard, garden and sometimes even the fields. With the aid of their children, they spun the wool or flax, wove cloth, made soap and candles, sewed and embroidered. The butter and eggs farm wives sold were an important source of income for the family. Vegetables and bread were also sold to railway gangs and bachelor farmers. The importance of the wife generally meant that women were highly sought after by men and that most widows quickly remarried.

Life for many women was hard. Productive farms required continuous investment, and extra money usually went to buy farm machinery. Consequently, as one observer has noted, "the modernization of many households lagged far behind the mechanization of field work. Long after the farm work had been taken over by horses and machines, many farm houses ran on woman power." In her article "The Decline of Women in Canadian Dairying," Marjorie Griffin Cohen points out that this pattern of failing to upgrade equipment for work done by women extended beyond the house to the barn as well. Initially women were responsible for taking care of the dairy cows and producing butter and cheese. The improvement of dairy technology accompanied the redefinition of dairying as work for men.

Not all women were farm wives, though in the days prior to the rapid growth of urban centres, family life in the village was not that much different than that on the farm. Some women, frequently younger ones, were in domestic service. There are records from the early nineteenth century of girls as young as seven being indentured until the age of eighteen. Older women, often widows, tended bar in taverns, acted as cooks in camps, took in washing, and in some cases ran boarding houses. Midwifery, of course, was the occupational preserve of women, but for most women their home was their workplace, where they performed the crucial roles of home production and family reproduction.

On Canada's east coast, where agriculture played a secondary role to fishing, women did participate more directly in the production of the market staple. The men worked the fisheries while the women worked on the shores, processing and dressing the fish. It is reported that some women could dress two to three thousand fish in a day. Still, women's reproductive role, not only in bearing children but in maintaining the family, was paramount, as children were equally important in production. It was known that not only could a woman help as much as another man but that the larger the family, the better the man did.

Early Industrialization

Beginning around the middle of the last century, Canada entered a period of economic transformation. The process began in southern Ontario and along the St. Lawrence River through western Quebec, though for many other parts of Canada the rise of industrialism and the decline of the family production unit would not take place until about the time of the Second World War, if not later. Even with the expansion of a market economy in the 1850s and 1860s in Central Canada, in the first stage of transformation, craft work remained centred in the home and the family was still the primary unit of production. Typically, men would weave with their sons as apprentices, while women and girls would spin. This pattern continued long after factories were built alongside the cottages of the craft workers. In the railway shops and machinery and metal plants, however, could be found the shape of things to come. The factory system began to predominate in the major industrial centres like Toronto and Montreal in the 1870s and 1880s.

Accompanying this change in the economic system was a shift in the population from the rural areas to the major urban centres. From 1851 to 1901 the population of Ontario doubled while that of Toronto increased sixfold. In the same period, Quebec's population also doubled but Montreal's population increased by four and a half times. The population of Winnipeg, the connecting link between the industrializing East and the western wheat economy, grew dramatically, by almost eighteenfold between 1881 and 1908. This was a period of massive immigration into the West, but also into central Canada, creating a vast pool of cheap labour for industry. Some people were also leaving their farms in the face of decreasing opportunities in the settled areas of Ontario and Quebec. Quebec in particular had a large surplus rural population, a factor which spurred heavy emigration to the textile mills and lumber camps of the northeastern United States. Young women also left the farms in increasing numbers, in part because the lack of agricultural opportunities meant little prospect of finding an appropriate husband. By 1871 women outnumbered men in Montreal in all age groups.

The shift from rural to urban areas was one manifestation of a much larger phenomenon, the increasing monetization of markets and its corollary, increased production for the market rather than for home consumption. Agricultural productivity rose with increased mechanization and new technology. The railways linked up rural and urban, city and town, bringing food to the market but also integrating markets, which allowed the growing factories to undercut the craftsmen located in towns and villages. Companies such as Eaton's used advertising and the mails to encourage women to buy ready-made clothing rather than make their own. Goods previously produced by the family now had to be bought, particularly as the population urbanized, creating the need for greater cash income. Work that had been done by women in the home was now done for employers in return for wages.

The flood of people to the cities, crowding around the industrial areas where work could be found, created appalling living conditions. Poverty was rampant, since wages were low and work unsteady. In the course of research for his 1897 study of Montreal, *City Below the Hill*, Herbert Ames discovered that one in every ten dwellings was a rear tenement, frequently in a state of decay, and over half the families were still using pit privies (outhouses). Greg Kealey and Michael Piva have documented similar conditions in Toronto around the same time. In some sections of Montreal, Ames found a population density as high as 300 people per acre, with five to eight people living in two rooms. In some of the poorest areas, the death rate was almost 50 per cent higher than the average. Almost an eighth of the population subsisted on less than what Ames considered a poverty income, a result, in the majority of cases, of the lack of or irregularity of work. Even when one family member was employed, the single wage was not usually sufficient to support a family, with the result that more than one member would have to work. The average family had 1.41 wage earners but the number varied depending on the occupation of the father. Bettina Bradbury's study of Montreal in 1871, for instance, showed that the average number of paid workers in a proprietor's family was 1.2 compared with 1.8 for semi-skilled and unskilled workers. Evidence before the Royal Commission on the Relations of Labour and Capital in 1889 showed that a cigar maker, a wife, and two or three children were barely able to live on the average salary of $7 a week. But the average pay reported by immigration agents for unskilled workers in the industrial towns of Central and Eastern Canada at the time was between $1.00 and $1.50 per day or $6 to $9 a week, if the worker was continuously employed. In 1889 a male labourer in Ontario averaged less than $6 a week; a cotton mill operative, under $7. In areas or times when unemployment was high, in winter when costs rose, or when the father was ill or disabled, it was essential that other members of the family went out to work.

✗ Women and children did go out to work and in large numbers. In 1871 women and "girls" made up 34.5 per cent, women and children 42 per cent, of the industrial work force in Montreal. By 1881, the proportion of industrial workers that was women and girls had risen to 37 per cent. In the clothing industry women and children comprised 80 per cent of the work force; in tobacco products, 60 per cent. By 1908 in the Quebec cotton industry, almost 50 per cent of the operatives in the factories were women. In Toronto in 1871, women and children made up over half of the workers in light manufacturing such as in clothing, shoes, printing, tobacco and furniture. They represented 34 per cent of the total industrial labour force. These figures, while indicating the importance of women in industry, must be seen in light of the fact that the vast majority were under the age of 25, indeed, mostly under 20. As Bradbury notes in her 1984 article, "for girls wage labour was a temporary and intermittent experience — something that they did at the most for four or five years, usually between the ages of 15 and 20." As a result, the percentage of women over ten years of age working for pay only rose to 11 per cent in 1891 and to 14 per cent in 1911 according to census figures. The comparable figures for men show an increase to 76 per cent and 79 per cent over the same period, though half of the men were employed in agriculture. Therefore, although the number of women working for pay was significant, the majority of women were not registered as gainfully employed. One consequence of this was that widows became heavily dependent on the income-earning capacity of their children rather than on wage work.

The shift to wage work did not immediately affect the family as a unit in many cases. Initially in the textile industry, the family unit was preserved by moving it out of the home and into the factory. Factories advertised for families even in the rural areas, offering the inducement that children would remain under the family's supervision while allowing the mother to earn an income, although this was really designed to get a whole family of workers for the price of one living wage. The low wages of the women and children were a great boon to the emergent industrialists. The companies also provided cottages near the factory to encourage families to work as a group. This continued until, later in the nineteenth century, the spread of public education, the enforcement of truancy laws, changes in work organization, and the passage and enforcement of factory laws kept younger children out of the mills.

Outside of family work units, women usually moved into jobs that were commercial counterparts to the work they had done in the home or on the farm. They would sew, clean, prepare food, teach, or keep boarders — jobs now done for pay where previously they had been done for the family. Women who had spun flax or wool produced on the family farm were now working in textile factories. Rather than cooking, baking and preserving for their families, women were working in biscuit factories. For example, by 1891 one-third of the biscuit and confectionery workers in Toronto were women. In her fascinating study of the Ganong Bothers factory in St. Stephen, New Brunswick, Margaret McCallum reported that by the turn of century two-thirds of the 200 confectionery workers employed by the factory were female, mostly young and single, a pattern not disturbed until the Second World War. Instead of sewing their children's clothing, women bought clothing from the companies they worked for. According to the Canadian census, the number of seamstresses increased more than tenfold between 1851 and 1871. The growth of markets and new technology created some new jobs heavily inhabited by women such as shop girls and telephone operators. In the latter case, women made up 61 per cent of Bell Telephone employees.

These women were, on the whole, poorly paid in relation to men, and were frequently subjected to fines and reductions in wages. Evidence before the 1889 Royal Commission on the Relations of Labour and Capital showed that Eaton's paid the average salesman $10 to $12 a week, while a first-class saleswoman could hope to make $6 to $8 a week. In the Kingston Cotton Company, women received 57 per cent of the average male wage. Ames conjectured in his study that the average wage was $8.25 per week for men, $4.50 for women; in other words women's wages were 55 per cent of men's. Three to five dollars a week was typical pay for women compared with $6 to $8 or $9 for unskilled males, though there were isolated examples of experienced laundry workers and skilled seamstresses who could make skilled workers' salaries in the $12-to-$18-a-week range by 1912. Still, in 1910 the average wage for women employed in manufacturing was only $5.44 per week, which was at or below minimum subsistence levels for a single person and only 57 per cent of the male average of $9.58.

Fines and other abuses of wages by companies reduced effective wages further. The 1889 royal commission found situations where fines were only levied on women and children. In one shoe company, young girls were paid 1¢ for every sole they made but were fined 4¢

for every defective sole. The manufacturer made a clear profit of 1¢ on every defective sole. At the Crompton Corset Company in Toronto where 230 of the 250 employees were women, workers were fined for mistakes on the basis of the time taken to rectify the mistake, but at a rate of 10¢ or 11¢ an hour, about $6 to $7 a week, even though they were paid only $5 a week in summer and $4.50 a week in the winter.

How common these abuses were is hard to say, but the practice of paying lower wages in winter, the off-season when unemployment was high, was common enough, though not restricted to women's work. The middle-class National Council of Women in 1900 explained that advertisements that promised linen would be hemmed free did not mean seamstresses were being paid starvation wages but rather that women were being given employment in the off-season. It was not unheard of, in fact it was apparently common in the Maritimes, for employers to be paid relief money as a wage subsidy, substantially reducing their wage bills. In any case, it is evident that employers took advantage of unemployment to pay even more inadequate wages.

Not only low wages afflicted women workers; they often worked incredibly long hours, commonly longer than men. In the dress trades, they might work regularly from eight in the morning to six at night, but until eleven or twelve at night in the rush season. For factory workers the average day was nine hours but some clerks in Montreal shops worked fifteen- or sixteen-hour days. Laws were passed in 1884 restricting the hours women could work to sixty hours a week in the factories, and the evidence of factory inspectors before the 1889 royal commission was that this limit was rarely exceeded except in the woollen mills, where sixty-six hours was common.

There were other ways, however, of abusing women besides the regular requirement of long hours. The royal commission also discovered that when machines broke down women had to work overtime without pay to make up the hours lost. A royal commission set up to investigate Bell Telephone after a strike in 1907 uncovered the fact that thirty-two operators a day in Toronto worked six and a half hours a day rather than the scheduled five. The schedule was rotated and no one received additional pay for the extra hours, while Bell, on the other hand, received forty-eight hours a day free. As well, on every five-hour shift, one "girl," as they were referred to, was expected to start work fifteen minutes early, then work the full shift, while a second worked fifteen minutes late. For every two operators,

Bell received a half hour of unpaid-for work. Why did women tolerate these wages and conditions? Simply because the alternatives were as bad or worse.

Moreover, in many industries, women were employed primarily as a "flexible" reserve of labour, hired only on a part-year basis in peak seasons. At the Ganong Brothers factory, for instance, almost two-thirds of the female workers worked less than half the year in 1931, two-fifths a quarter year or less. On the other hand, among the male employees, over half were employed full-year or substantially full-year (ten months or more). Less than 20 per cent were employed for three months or less.

Domestic work was one alternative to industrial work in the late nineteenth century, but it was considered the least desirable occupation by most. In 1891 domestics made up 41 per cent of the female work force, by 1921 only 18 per cent. As early as the 1870s there were complaints about the shortage of domestics because young women were going to work in the factories instead. It is not hard to understand why when one looks at the working conditions. In the 1880s in Eastern Canada, wages of domestics ranged from $4 to $10 a month, $10 to $20 a month in Western Canada. By the end of the century, the rate had risen in the East to $8 to $14 a month but remained much the same in the West. With room and board, wages were comparable with factory work but this did not compensate for the fact that domestic work was lonely and menial, the hours were long, and there was always the chance of sexual abuse (though this was also all too common in the factory). To remedy the shortage, unattached female relatives were taken in as free domestics, and immigrant women were brought in to work as servants. By 1911, 35 per cent of all domestic servants were immigrants. In her article, "The Women Ontario Welcomed: Immigrant Domestics for Ontario Homes, 1870-1930," Marilyn Barber writes that between Confederation and the depression over a quarter of a million women immigrated to Canada with the intention of working as a domestic.

Why were female wages so low? The overstocking of the labour market with women, children and unskilled immigrants meant that the employers could get away with low pay. Women and children had to work in order to produce a living family wage. On the other hand, employers took advantage of this situation to justify low wages. Young working women were living with their families and therefore did not need a living wage. To both the 1889 royal commission and the one investigating Bell Telephone, employers asserted that they preferred to hire "girls" who lived at home. Cotton mill owners admitted in 1899 that girls were expected to live at home since it was unlikely they could manage paying board at $3 per week when their wage might be only $3 or $4 a week. The operating manager for Bell in Toronto stated that the company did not pay a sufficient wage to meet the cost of living, so the 30 to 40 per cent of the operators who boarded had to work overtime or at a second job. Despite this, as early as 1868 there were as many as 5,000 "girls" living on their own in Toronto. As late as 1912, one Toronto writer described the difficulties of an independent woman attempting to live on a wage of $5 a week when meals cost $2.25 and a room $1.50, leaving just $1.25 for all other expenses, including clothes.

Most of these women were young, whether they lived at home or on their own, and they did not usually stay in the work force for long. Bell paid extra wage benefits to operators who stayed for more than two or three years, but the average stay of an operator was still less than three years. Most women who worked in the factories were young, between fifteen and twenty years old, and they tended to leave after a few years to get married, as indeed they virtually had to do in order to survive. This rapidly overturning, unorganized work force provided a large pool of cheap labour for employers; and, not incidentally, they also provided another generation of cheap labour, subsidized by pooled family income.

In his study of Montreal, Ames documented the make-up of the family work force which reflected women's role as secondary wage earners. He calculated that in an average 30 families there would be 147 people, 42 wage earners, 46 hometenders, 10 lodgers, 27 school-age children and 22 infants. He did not document how many of the lodgers he recorded were men or women, which might have given some indication of the number of single women living independently. However, most lodgers were probably men because of the unequal sex ratio indicated in his family statistics. The wage earners would be made up of 33 men, 8 women, and 1 child. Of the twelve families with a second wage earner, only three would have a second male working. The other nine families would have a woman or child working. Women, therefore, obviously played an important role as secondary wage earners, and they were probably mostly daughters, since in 1871 only 2.5 per cent of wives reported any income, though this certainly understates wives' contribution to family income through non-wage work.

Within the home, women turned home work into paid work by

sewing at piece rates, by cleaning for someone else or by taking in lodgers; however, this was almost never recognized in census statistics. Fathers and sons would work in the factories while mothers and daughters would work at home sewing. The sweating system, where women sewed for piece rates and were paid as little as possible, was used by employers to undercut other contractors at the women's expense. Sewing in the home did, however, make looking after children possible. Bradbury found that 45 per cent of women in 1871 who sewed at home in the St. Jacques district of Montreal had children under the age of five.

Taking in boarders or sharing the home with another family was an alternative way of increasing family income or cutting home costs. When the children were young and the mother was unable to work outside the home, the family was most likely to share their home. Ames reported that nine in ten families shared their homes with another family, while every third family was also likely to have a boarder. In one section of the city, he discovered that 20 per cent of the population were boarders. Having boarders was an alternative to going out to do domestic work and allowed women to be their own boss and to care for their children.

When women were forced to support themselves and their families, hardship and poverty were frequent companions because women's wages or home work earnings were paid as if the women were secondary wage earners. Of the families Ames classed as poor, 36 per cent were relying on women as the primary wage earner. The poverty that resulted was reflected in the reported cases of starvation, indigence, and the abandonment of babies, or their placement in orphanages. The influx of immigrants and rural people and the need for secondary wage earners provided a surplus labour supply for the employer, so neither women nor men usually earned a "family" wage. The degradation of women's wages left them with a further disadvantage when trying to support a family.

The New Occupations

Not all women's work that emerged from industrialization was menial, unskilled or directly related to domestic work. The expansion of compulsory public education required a major expansion in the number of teachers. Initially there was a debate over the appropriateness of hiring women, whether it was proper for women to teach in public even though they had taught for many years privately in homes. Eventually it was accepted that women could teach and discipline the younger children. It was considered acceptable for women to look after children in their tender years, but at the secondary level male teachers were considered necessary to mould young men into shape for the labour market. It can be argued that women's teaching at the elementary level was just the extension of the mothers' teaching role in the home, but perhaps more plausible is the argument that cost was the deciding factor. Women would work for less money than men, though men were still retained to teach in secondary schools.

By 1897, 421 out of 445 teachers in Toronto were women but their pay was considerably less than men's. Women teachers were paid as little as a third of the income of their male counterparts in Eastern Canada, somewhat better in the West. In the Toronto School Division in 1858, school masters made $700 a year, headmistresses $400. On the basis of the then prevailing wage scales it would take a woman fourteen years to reach the male starting salary, but by this time it was expected that women would have left teaching to be married. Married women were not considered appropriate as teachers. The Toronto board went as far as passing a motion in 1895 prohibiting the hiring of married women or women over thirty on the assumption that they should be at home tending their families!

There were several factors behind the low salaries. Women could enter college at sixteen, two years younger than men, and did not have to take the same exams. Lower wages were then justified on the basis that women were less qualified than men. Secondly, there was a surplus of women applicants. With few work alternatives for educated women, one-half of women graduates entered teaching. In 1900 the National Council of Women reported the result:

> The teaching profession is overcrowded and the prospects cheerless. Teachers are overworked and underpaid and there is comparatively little hope of advancement for even the most talented Canadian women teachers.

Boards also maintained that young women would leave after a few years just as they were becoming experienced and therefore were not worth the investment of a large salary. Under the prevailing rules in Toronto where women over thirty who did not quit were let go anyway, this excuse at best has a hollow ring to it.

Still, teaching was the most important opportunity for women in the professions. By 1911 women comprised about half of all professionals and most of these women were teachers. Those who studied in the other professions such as medicine and law were few in number due to university regulations, and what is more, provincial laws usually prevented them from practising. The only other opportunity for educated middle-class women was charitable or religious work.

Other white-collar occupations were just beginning to open up to women. Shop clerking offered the greatest opportunities. Four per cent of working women were in merchandising occupations in 1891, but within twenty years this had risen to 12 per cent (though women still only represented 15 per cent of the total labour force in trade occupations). The numbers were, however, significant in the larger centres. Secretarial work still remained primarily a male preserve, though women were increasingly attending commercial colleges. Only one in fifty employed women worked at clerical work in 1891, just a few thousand in the whole of Canada. By 1911 this number had increased eightfold.

The Reform Movement and "Working Women"

As in Britain and other countries the brutality of the industrial revolution brought to the fore middle-class reform movements, one of their prime goals being to protect women and children from the excesses of the factory system through limiting the hours women could work and through restricting child labour. Previously, children had been expected to work as part of the family unit, but by the end of the century reformers were more concerned with the child's right to a childhood. Factory acts were introduced in Ontario in 1883 and in Quebec two years later. The acts were hardly rigorous. Girls under fourteen and boys under twelve were prohibited from working in factories; but small shops were excluded from this restriction, and enforcement was lax, allowing employers to avoid the law. In this they were aided and abetted by some parents who needed the extra source of income and by certificates of exemption which parents could routinely request. However, gradually more and more children did leave the factories and increased their school attendance. The result was a mixed blessing for working-class families. The woman's role as reproducer of the family production unit, so important in pre-industrial and early-industrial society, was undermined. It was not until the 1920s, according to David Millar's estimates, that male incomes of the unskilled reached the level of a living family wage. The family still needed secondary wage earners to support itself but children were now largely excluded from filling this role. This meant that that role increasingly fell to wives.

Reformers were disturbed by the results. When J.S. Woodsworth examined the state of the family in urban communities at the end of the first decade of this century, he found that mothers had been forced to go into the work force to replace the earnings of children. The primary reason given by girls for dropping out of the school was that they had to take care of younger children at home, which led these same reformers to lament parental neglect and the lack of child discipline. Agitation for day care was one answer, and even the orphanages were used as temporary child-care centres.

However, there was more to the reformers' concern than just the exploitation by industrial employers, particularly of girls, through low pay and long hours. They sought to keep young girls out of the work force or in better work situations out of a concern for the morality of the girls and their role in reproduction rather than out of a concern for wages. Woodsworth thought girls and young women would be coarsened by working in factories. Others thought factory work especially detrimental because of its perceived effect in destroying a woman's "womanliness" and, more important to the patrimony, in making her less anxious to be a wife and mother. The health of women was a concern because of the expectation that they would become wives and mothers. The royal commission on the 1907 Bell strike was critical of the employment practices because the commissioners considered them detrimental to the health of young women. The National Council of Women was especially glad to see the Ontario Shops Act passed, which required seating for shop girls, since it was thought that prolonged standing would hurt their reproductive organs. It is questionable if all this concern with morality and health was really at the root of reformer campaigns. At least one major concern was that female economic independence would undermine the prevailing patriarchal system. Canadian governmental opposition to women registering homesteads was based on the fear that women would become too independent and fail to fill their expected role as reproducers of the labour force.

The reformers also failed to examine the reasons why women

worked and why their wages were so poor. In some ways, despite their good intentions, the reforms hurt women by excluding them from the industrial labour force or by making them uncompetitive. Prior to the reforms, children, including young girls, and men worked in the factories, while mothers took care of the home. After the reforms women and men worked while the young girls stayed at home with the children. Rather than improving the living standards of the family, reforms tended only to shift the responsibilities of the work at home from mothers to daughters. In both cases the employer benefited by paying wages that were part of a family wage.

The Trades and Labour Congress (TLC) also advocated that women be excluded from work in the factories to preserve male jobs and wages, and would often appeal to concerns about their morality and health. A quarter of a century later during the depression, the same issues surfaced again. Almost certainly with the labour unions the issue was wages; not women's wages, but men's. The large supply of cheap female labour helped to keep all wages low.

Work in the home may not have been paid, but it was critical to the support and reproduction of the family. A contemporary observer noted, for instance, how girls who lived at home could afford to live on their wages because they received such things as free laundering, cooking, and living space. The benefit of this unpaid work went to the employer, who got more work than he paid for, while the burden was shouldered by the working-class wife. This conclusion did not escape the royal commissioners investigating the strike at Bell Telephone:

> To the extent to which the Bell Telephone Company has profited by the necessities of its operators, or has secured services at a rate which would not have enabled those who rendered them to have lived, but for the support received from members of their own families, or in ways other than those provided by the company, to this extent the profits of the company have been derived by a species of sweating, or by the levying of a tax upon homes and individuals for which no compensation has been made.

War, Depression, and War

The second phase of the industrial revolution in Canada was drawing to a close in the years just prior to the First World War. Reform was restricting women's access to factory work, but that was probably much less important than the third phase of industrial change, the emergence of large corporations and the administrative revolution that followed. In the 1890s the process was well under way in the United States and, to a lesser extent, in Britain. In Canada the full impact was not felt until the first great merger movement from 1907 to 1912 when a number of giant Canadian firms were created by joining together smaller, previously competitive, firms. The process would be continued in the twenties with enormous impact on women's paid work, particularly in the resulting rise of the clerical trades. Even by 1911 some effects were evident. Nine per cent of women workers were clerks, up from just over two per cent in 1891. Production work on the other hand, was increasingly male-dominated except in some of the traditional light industries like clothing and textiles. The service occupations, teaching and health care, were the havens for women workers in the transition.

For much of Canada, the upheaval we have described in women's work in the late nineteenth century was as distant as it was to the families of Ontario in the 1820s. With the new century, however, the woman's role as partner in the family enterprise, albeit a subordinate partner, was rapidly disappearing. Although the farms of the Prairies remained family concerns, in the regional urban centres like Winnipeg, Vancouver and Halifax the family production unit was destroyed to a greater or lesser extent as the market invaded the home. And in the primary sector comparable developments were underway. The mines and forest industries of the resource hinterlands never did employ women. Women living in these areas had to look to other places to augment the family income. The B.C. fishing industry was capitalist from the start, and women worked in the canning factories, as they did in the fish-processing plants of the Atlantic, as secondary wage earners. It is perhaps significant that the relative wage levels of women through the industrial revolution in Central Canada and, to a lesser extent, in the Maritimes remained consistently between 55 and 60 per cent of male wages — significant in the sense that throughout Canada, the differential remained more or less unchanged over the following century. The market did nothing to diminish systemic discrimination.

The outbreak of the First World War in 1914 brought very little immediate change to the Canadian labour market. The economy was still in the throes of a depression which began in 1912, and the ranks of enlisted men were readily filled without the mobilization of women workers. Conscription was not introduced until late in the war as well. Despite the Imperial War Board's encouragement to employers to use women in non-traditional factory work, therefore, there was little need to do so and women were still registering as unemployed until well into the hostilities. In a thesis written in 1919, investigating changes in the occupations of women, Enid Price revealed that during the war most factories that lost men to the armed forces generally replaced them with other men or did not replace them at all. This policy was encouraged by the craft unions, which feared dilution of their skills and the devaluation of their members' work.

As the war dragged on and mobilization increased, the labour market began to tighten up and by 1916 the economy began to approach full employment. Many factories were switched over to produce munitions for the Imperial Munitions Board, and in these factories women began to fill positions. While there were no women among the 6,000 munitions workers in 1915 in Montreal, by 1917 35 per cent of the 15,000 employed were women. Their wages, as might be expected, lagged well behind those of the men. Women's wages in the munitions industry ranged between twenty and thirty-five cents per hour, or approximately between 50 and 80 per cent of those of men. As the war began to draw to a close, however, the women workers were beginning to be replaced by returning soldiers and other men; consequently, by 1918 women's share of employment in the industry had fallen to 22 per cent of the work force. Relative wages had shown some improvement, on the other hand, to between twenty-one cents and forty-five cents per hour or 60 to 80 per cent of the average male wage.

The relatively small increase in the number of women participating in the labour force is reflected in the fact that the composition of women workers as measured by marital status did not change appreciably. Women workers were largely unmarried, 80 per cent being single, and only 15 per cent of them were entering employment for the first time. Most moved from other factories into the munitions plants or stayed on when their factories were converted over, although there was some movement from less lucrative traditional women's occupations. Price, for instance, found that 6 per cent had formerly worked in domestic service.

In factories where traditional work remained, such as the clothing plants and textile mills, the role of women changed even less than in the munitions plants. While they may have replaced men for a while on some of the machines, the changes were generally temporary. The reason, according to Price, was that even when conscription was introduced, many of the men working in these factories were ineligible. Either they were not of military age, they were married, or, very importantly in areas with large numbers of immigrant workers, they were not Canadian citizens. The only new industry that was hiring women in significant numbers was the rubber goods industry where they were sufficiently well regarded that employers wished to keep them on even when the soldiers returned. We suspect a major inducement was the prevailing lower female wage.

Though there was not a large change in female participation in non-traditional jobs in the primary and secondary industries, there were more substantive effects on tertiary employment and particularly in clerical occupations, effects that persisted after the war. Price found for Montreal that while the number of clerical workers dropped by 20 per cent from 1914 to 1918, the number of women in these occupations rose by 50 per cent. Women had represented 15 per cent of clerical workers in 1914 but 30 per cent in 1918. As well, their income rose substantially, from $47 a month to $90, and in relation to men, from 60 per cent of the male salary to 85 per cent.

The substitution of women clerks for men occurred in a number of industries. In wholesale houses where men were assumed to be needed to lift heavy containers, clerical work passed to women as enlistment rapidly depleted the ranks of male labourers and office workers and the remaining men were shifted to the heavier work. An interesting feature, if somewhat atypical, was the fact that women took these places at equal pay.

Women working in the railway shops were not so fortunate. In 1914 they made up only 3 per cent of the clerical work force, although, surprisingly, they earned 4 per cent more than men. By 1918, however, they comprised 30 per cent of the work force but were making only 80 to 90 per cent of the male salary.

These shifts in clerical work from a traditional male domain to a female one are only examples of a larger trend which was under way even before the war but undoubtedly accelerated by it. By 1911 women already comprised a third of all clerical workers; by 1921 their proportion was over 40 per cent. The percentage of women workers in clerical occupations doubled over that decade, reaching almost one out of every five by 1921. No comparable increase was achieved before or after this period until the Second World War.

Banks and retail outlets also turned to the female labour force during the First World War. In Montreal the number of female bank clerks rose from 12.5 per cent in 1914 to 42 per cent in 1918. The Royal Bank of Canada alone had hired almost three times as many women by 1916 as it had employed in 1914. Starting salaries rose over the same period from $400 to $600 a year, no doubt reflecting the tightness of the labour market and rising inflation. Apparently, the monetary inducement was successful, since 54 per cent of the women working as clerks by 1918 were working at their first paid job.

In retail trade the expansion was less dramatic but nevertheless significant. Women took temporary jobs as sales clerks despite twelve-and-a-half-hour work days. There were reportedly 12,000 of them in Canada late in the war, almost half of them in Toronto. Most were young and single, between eighteen and twenty-two years old.

These changes in women's paid work, with the exception of the rise of the clerical trades, were to prove transitory. After the war the proportion of women working and the areas in which they worked largely reverted back to pre-war characteristics. However, there were some significant changes — at least working conditions had improved over what they had been a decade or two earlier. Hours of paid work for women declined slightly from those at the turn of the century, from around sixty to fifty-two to fifty-five hours a week. The average age of women workers also rose as an increasing proportion of women over twenty-five entered the work force and fewer and fewer girls between ten and nineteen. However, the decline in the number of young girls does not seem to indicate they were going to school. In his study of Montreal, *Anatomy of Poverty*, Terry Copp comes to the conclusion that many stayed at home to look after the younger children while their mothers went out to work.

This movement towards older women in the work force corresponds with the drop in the relative importance of female factory work, a longtime work area for young, single women, which was particularly evident in the twenties. Between 1921 and 1931, the percentage of women working in manufacturing dropped from 18 to 13 per cent, while those working in the service industry and in clerical jobs rose from 46 to 52 per cent. The composition of service work was likewise changing. Women working in domestic service dropped from 42 per cent in 1901 to 26 per cent in 1921 and continued falling in subsequent decades.

Despite the fierce depression in the early years of the twenties, some real gains were made by labour even in the face of the virtual destruction of the organized labour movement. A number of minimum wage acts were established, with Manitoba and B.C. leading the way in 1918 (though perhaps the most important effect was to put a floor under male wages rather than benefit women directly). Quebec, Saskatchewan, Nova Scotia and Ontario followed in 1920. Women were not involved in the regulatory commissions established, however, and the wage levels set were inadequate and in any case did not cover home, farm or piece work. The only other protective legislation was the implementation in 1921 of a six-week maternity leave in British Columbia.

Economic changes that had begun before the war re-emerged in the later twenties when a second merger wave furthered the rise of corporate capitalism with its application of principles of scientific management, job stratification and, in response to the labour upheavals after the war, measures of corporate welfarism — principles applied not only to the production floor but to the increasing corporate bureaucracies. The result, as one student of the process has noted, "was a highly rationalized office in which deskilled jobs were defined as suitable women's work." The triumph of industrialism was not without its benefits. Real wages did improve and male wages rose sufficiently to constitute a living family wage.

Neither protective legislation, industrial growth nor higher real wages, however, proved any protection against the ravages of the Great Depression of the thirties. Production fell dramatically, unemployment rose to around a quarter of the labour force, and wages fell. Wage rates by 1931 were already below the levels of 1921. Women were especially hurt, as they tended to be the first let go. Less skilled and less organized than men, they were easy victims. There was a particular social opposition to married women working because it was seen as a threat to the jobs of men and their ability to support families. Indeed, Ruth Roach Pierson notes that except during the wartime period when there was a shortage of qualified teachers and civil servants, "the policy of most school boards and provincial and municipal civil services as well as of the federal government itself (until 1955), was to require women to relinquish their positions at marriage or, alternatively, at first pregnancy."

This attitude towards married women was exemplified in the debate over the various unemployment insurance plans proposed in 1935, 1938 and 1940, and in the actual provisions of the one finally adopted in 1940. The basic assumption underpinning the entire debate was that women were either "single, independent working women" (young women, not yet married), or "dependent wives/mothers." Since the former would have no dependents and the latter were assumed to be looked after by a male receiving a "family wage," the Unemployment Insurance scheme, in Pierson's words "sought to preserve, not eliminate, wage differentials of both class and gender.... [W]omen's principal access to benefit was to be through the indirect channel of dependants' allowances.... [which served] to enforce their dependence [rather] than to entitle dependent wives and children to adequate provision."

Women's wages were equally open to attack. An example of what happened to women can be found in the experience of women working for Eaton's in Toronto, which led in part to the establishment of the Royal Commission on Price Spreads. By 1935 some women were making as little as $6.00 to $7.00 a week despite the fact that $12.50 was the established minimum subsistence level for women living on their own. Piecework rates for dressmakers had been reduced by more than 50 per cent, to $1.75 for twelve dresses after 1933 from the previous level of $3.60. Women also faced an extension in hours; it is estimated that on average they worked more than 10 per cent longer hours than men, though female wages remained between 50 and 60 per cent of male wages, continuing the pattern of a half century earlier.

The Second World War prompted a dramatic turn-around in the economy and with it a relief from some of labour's problems. As men left the work camps and relief lines to become soldiers and industry started to expand again, women entered the labour market in large numbers. The number of working women grew from 638,000 in 1939 to 1,077,000 by October of 1944, a growth of 69 per cent. Women were offered incentives to entice them into the labour market, including day care, tax breaks, and a registration and referral service offered by the National Selective Service. (The NSS was established in 1942 when it became obvious that the pools of unemployed from the depression had completely dried up.) The NSS's appeal to women's patriotism was hardly necessary after a decade of depression. A survey of women over thirty-five who were working (the least likely group to be in the labour force) found that only 9 per cent were working out of patriotism. The majority, 60 per cent, gave money as their reason.

For the same monetary reason women left their traditional areas of work to enter the war industries where they received higher pay. One result was a rising shortage of labour in the service industries, hospitals, restaurants and hotels. The NSS responded with an aggressive campaign to recruit women into the work force. Young, single women were the prime target of this campaign, followed by childless married women, and, finally, married women with children. All women between twenty and twenty-four years of age (excepting nuns, the sick or the criminal) were registered. The problem the agency encountered was that the young, single group targeted as the first reserve of labour had already been largely utilized in the industrially developed areas. Concentration was then shifted to encourage unmarried women to move from the less-developed and rural areas to where jobs were available.

The campaigns were vigorous and aggressive. Female industrial workers were paraded. Advertisements, demonstrations and even fashion shows of factory clothing were used to encourage women to seek employment in the factories — except in Quebec where the politicians feared that the public was still too socially conservative to accept the idea of a working mother. Campaigns were tailor-made to fit the needs of a particular area. In Ottawa, for instance, there was an appeal to former civil servants to work in the government war offices.

As the recruitment proceeded and women with children were involved, the issues of child care and women's position as tax deductions on their husbands' incomes had to be resolved to entice women into the labour market. The federal government moved to solve these problems with an offer of cost-sharing with the provinces for day care and changes in the income tax act. Under the day-care provisions twenty-eight new day nurseries were established in Ontario and five in Quebec, hardly a major program. Under the tax revisions husbands retained their wives' marriage exemption regardless of the wives' earnings. These concessions were only temporary, however.

As the men returned from the front and went back to their old jobs, women were informed that their obligation was finished. The federal government stopped funding day care, and most of the centres — including all the Quebec centres — disappeared. The tax law was also changed, putting a limit of $250 a year on the amount a woman could earn without affecting her husband's deductions. It would appear from the complaints of employers that it was this tax measure that encouraged many married women to once again leave the labour market or to restrict themselves to part-time work, leaving the field to young, single women.

The Postwar Period

Despite the experience of women in the labour market during both wars, there is little evidence that it comprised much more than a temporary, war-induced aberration. Female participation rates in 1951 were only marginally higher than in 1941 and still well under one-quarter of the potential female labour force. Most were still young and single and concentrated in the same narrow range of occupations. As after the First World War, however, the growth in clerical occupations expanded, more than three times as rapidly as the labour force generally, and women made up the majority of this increase. By 1951 more than one out of every four employed women were classed as clerical and they comprised 57 per cent of all clerical workers, a rise from 50 per cent a decade earlier. The growth of corporate capitalism had been given considerable impetus by wartime mobilization and the postwar boom.

At the same time, wartime labour demand and the introduction of capital-intensive technology was causing a revolution on the farm. Between 1941 and 1951, the number of occupied farms in Canada fell 15 per cent. Five years later the number had fallen a further 8 per cent. Urbanization and the decline of the family production unit accelerated, creating the conditions for the revolution in women's labour market participation that took off in the sixties and seventies. The stage was set for the contemporary era.

2

Participation in the Workplace

The historical record of women's work in Canada up until the contemporary era gives considerable support to the contention that women have suffered from an inferior economic position in the labour market relative to that of most working men. This is not to say that life was ever very easy for most men but, in addition to the basic struggle for a living wage and decent working conditions, women suffered from a further double burden, discrimination in the labour market and responsibility for the bulk of work in the home.

The postwar period, and the sustained economic growth that occurred up until the stagflation of the seventies, have commonly been thought to have produced a major social and economic transformation in North American society. Rising per capita incomes and the spread of mass consumption led the prominent economist John Kenneth Galbraith to declare America *The Affluent Society* as early as 1958. But while incomes were growing, they were not growing equally; while opportunities were expanding, they were not open to all. The result was social unrest, particularly in the sixties, which spawned the civil rights movement, the war on poverty and a massive expansion of the education system. In Canada it also prompted the spread of unionism to the public sector and a substantial expansion in social programs. As evidenced by the appointment of the Royal Commission on the Status of Women, it also brought forward a new feminist movement critical of the restricted economic and career opportunities available in the workplace and the general repression of women in a male-dominated society. The problem was deemed particularly acute because of the rapid rise in female participation in the labour force, a rise that contributed to the image of the "new working woman." The unresolved question, however, is, have the social, legislative and economic changes of the last few decades really changed the income and employment opportunities for women?

Female Participation

We will leave consideration of the first aspect of the question, income opportunities, to the next chapter. As to the second, employment opportunities have changed in number, though not markedly in type, and changed quite dramatically in recent years. There has been a steady increase in this century in the proportion of women working for pay rather than working only as unpaid labour in the household (Figure 2-1). The increase was slow but was constant in the earlier years of this century. In the last few decades, however, this trickle has become a flood. The increase in participation rates in both the sixties and seventies equalled the total increase in the previous six decades, from 1901 to 1961. In the eighties, the rate of change moderated only slightly with the participation rate increase averaging almost two thirds of a percentage point per year.

Figure 2-1 Female Participation Rates

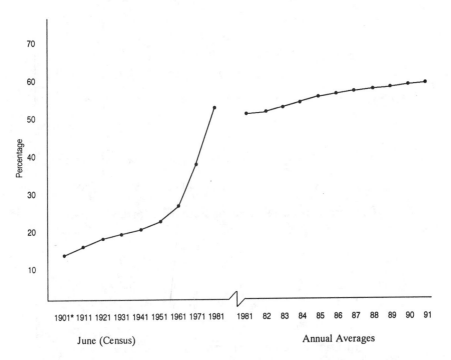

* 14 years of age and older in 1901; all other years 15 years and older
Source: 1901-1981: Census; 1981-1991: Statistics Canada,The Labour Force,
Annual Averages (71-001; 71-220)

By the nineties, six out of every ten women were in the labour market, (though with economic recession, free trade restructuring, the disappearance of many jobs and the consequent high unemployment, the increase in female participation rates dropped precipitously late in the decade, averaging only 0.15 per cent between 1989 and 1991. However, male participation rates in the same period fell by almost 2 per cent). Moreover, there has been a very significant change in the characteristics of women working in the labour market. In the early years of the century the vast majority of women in paid work were single, a high percentage in the fifteen to twenty-four age group. That is, they entered the labour market until marriage and family-rearing responsibilities took them out of the market and into the home. This remained true even by mid-century. In the great surge of female participation over the last thirty years, however, this pattern has greatly altered. Over 60 per cent of the married women in Canada are now in the labour force, and in 1991 they represented just over 64 per cent of total female income earners (see Table 2-1).

Table 2-1
Participation Rates of Women by Marital Status

Status	1951	1975	1980	1991
Single	58.1	59.2	63.3	66.5
Married	11.2	41.6	48.9	61.4
Other (widowed, divorced, separated)	19.3	31.5	34.8	35.7*
Total (15+ years)	24.0	44.4	50.3	58.2
Percentage of Female Labour Force by Marital Status				
Single	62.0	31.0	29.9	25.6
Married	30.0	59.6	59.9	64.2
Other	7.9	9.4	10.2	10.2
Total	100.0	100.0	100.0	100.0

(* The participation rate for divorced and separated only, excluding widowed, was 64.0, just slightly below the rate for married women.)
Sources: 1951 *Census*; Statistics Canada, *The Labour Force* (71-001); *The Labour Force, Annual Averages 1991* (71-220).

This influx of married women into the labour force has significantly changed the age structure of female workers. In earlier years the predominant pattern was for women to enter the labour market until they married or became pregnant, at which point they would leave the labour force. After the family had grown up, a significant number would re-enter the market, giving the pattern of female participation the typical "saddle" shape (Figure 2-2). By the mid-seventies, however, this pattern had changed. Fewer and fewer women were leaving the labour force to get married or raise a family. The saddle had disappeared. By 1991 all trace of the reproduction function had disappeared with participation rates peaking in the major family-rearing age categories, 25-44 years. Female participation patterns are more and more approaching male labour participation patterns.

Figure 2-2 Female Participation Rates by Age

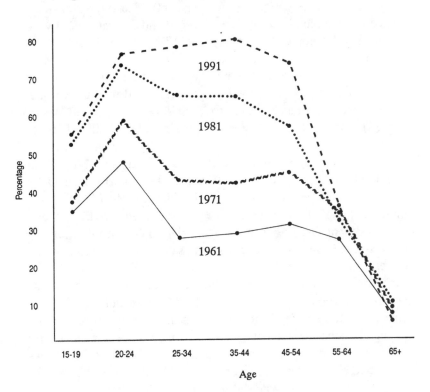

Source: 1961-1971: Census (June Figures); 1981-1991: Statistics Canada, The Labour Force Annual Averages (71-001; 71-220)

In short, there has been a revolution in women's labour market participation in the last three decades, a revolution marked by rapid increases in total female participation, most particularly among married women between the ages of twenty-four and fifty-five. What lies behind this revolution?

Why the Increase in Female Participation?

It has been generally true for the last century that a large proportion of single women, except perhaps for the daughters of the middle and upper classes, have worked either to support themselves or to contribute to the support of their families. The participation rate of single female children (age fifteen plus) still living in the family was just over 63 per cent by 1991 and fast approaching the comparable rate for male children (67.7 per cent). The figure for unattached women (single, widowed, divorced and separated not living in families) is somewhat lower, just 47.2, still well below the comparable male rate and, in fact, falling slightly from the rate a decade earlier. Adding to this number the female heads of households, 1,484,000 by 1991, over 44 per cent of all working women were without husbands (unmarried, widowed, separated or divorced). Included in this were approximately 700,000 female-headed, single-parent families, the number of which has multiplied in recent decades. According to the 1990 Gunderson, Muszynski and Keck study, single parent families, the majority headed by women, were 6 per cent of all families in 1961. By 1986 this had more than doubled, to 13 per cent. With rates of divorce and separation approaching a third of marriage rates and the trend to more single women having and keeping their children (15 per cent of female-headed single parent families in 1986), the number of such families is increasing and is bound to continue to do so. These are women who must work to support themselves and their dependents. The alternative — to rely on usually insufficient welfare payments, support payments, widows' pensions or some other form of transfer payment — is a recipe for poverty. Gunderson, Muszynski and Keck, for example, report that in 1986 the rate of poverty for single parent mothers who did not work in the labour market was 62.3 per cent. For the most part, therefore, single women work just to put bread upon the table.

Nevertheless, it is not non-married women who have accounted for the largest part of the tremendous upsurge in female participation. This is illustrated by the dramatic increase in two-earner families and the corresponding decrease in families where only the husband worked (reported in the same poverty study). In 1961, 65 per cent of all families were traditional "male breadwinner" families. By 1986 this had fallen to 12 per cent. Over the same period, families with both spouses working increased from 14 per cent to 52 per cent. The explanation for this increase is not so straightforward. Three explanations have been advanced in the economic literature. The first is economic — women need to enter the work force in order to maintain the real income of the family, particularly in a period of steadily rising prices, falling real incomes and rising tax burdens, or to purchase goods considered necessities due to rising expectations or social pressures. In addition, with continuous high unemployment, more married women need to work in order to guarantee a measure of family income security. Finally, since much of our social security benefits — pensions, dental plans, supplemental health plans, disability pensions — are tied to paid employment, many women need to work as insurance against family breakup, or death, disablement or unemployment of a spouse.

The second explanation frequently put forward is social. Increasing numbers of married women want to enter the labour market either because smaller families and labour-saving household appliances have, for some, made household work less time-consuming or less fulfilling, or because higher educational attainment by women has led to higher expectations of income, of job satisfaction, and of having a career.

A third, similar, argument advanced by economists is that rising real wages in the labour market make it more attractive for women to leave the home for paid work even though part of their income must be used for day care, cleaning services, fast foods, extra clothing, and other work-related expenses, and despite the fact that they must work at two jobs, one paid and one unpaid. Unstated in these explanations is the obvious possibility that women may want to enter the labour force for the independence that an income and career can provide. The abolition of universality in family allowances will only serve to increase this effect since women living in middle-income families will now be forced into the labour market if they wish to receive any income independent of their spouses.

What evidence can be marshalled in support of these three arguments? Evidence for 1971 presented in the first edition of Women and Work showed that participation rates of married women declined steadily as their husband's income rose, which strongly suggested that many married women are induced into the labour market because of the low income of their spouse. The evidence from the 1986 Census (Table 2-2) is less clear. Female participation did peak in the lower, but not the lowest, husband's income class and declined thereafter as the husband's income rose. What is perhaps more indicative of need is that it peaked at a lower income and was substantially higher overall for women with children, particularly pre-school children. These figures underestimate the effect that low spouse income has in propelling women into the labour market because, as Table 2-3 shows, women with higher levels of education have higher levels of labour market participation and women with higher levels of education tend to marry men with similar educational status and, hence, higher incomes. This means that if all women had the same educational level, the effect of spouses' income on women's participation would be much greater than that shown in Table 2-2.

Table 2-2
Participation Rates of Women with Husband/Partner Present, by Husband's Income, 1985

Participation Rates (%)

Husband's Income	Total	Children Present	No Children Present
Under $10,000	46.9	56.8	38.2
$10,000 -19,999	53.9	61.6	45.4
$20,000 -29,999	63.0	64.6	60.1
$30,000 -39,999	62.0	61.6	62.9
$40,000 -49,999	60.3	60.4	60.0
$50,000 -59,999	57.5	58.3	55.1
$60,000 and over	54.9	56.8	50.2
All incomes	57.3	61.2	50.8

Source: Patricia Connelly and Martha MacDonald, *Women in the Labour Force*, Table 3.

Table 2-3
Female Participation Rates by Educational Attainment, 1991

Education	%
0-8 years	22.7
9-13 years (high school)	55.7
Some post-secondary	68.7
Post-secondary certificate/diploma	73.1
University	80.4
All categories	58.2

Source: Statistics Canada, *The Labour Force, Annual Averages, 1991* (71-220)

The effect of spouses' income on participation should be expected: if the husband makes a low income, is unemployed or disabled, there is strong pressure on the wife to go out to work to supplement the monthly paycheck. Thus the low participation rates of women with the two lowest husband's incomes categories is perhaps surprising. However, it is in large measure explained by the fact that these categories include many older and retired people whose participation rates, male and female, are very low, rather than the younger women who have higher participation rates. For example, women with young children and a husband with income in the $10,000–$19,999 category have the highest female participation rate of all groups, at 66 per cent.

But husband's income does not explain why married women's participation rates are rising over time across all income categories. If the husband's real income has been rising over time, logic suggests that there has been less pressure, not more, on wives of men at the lower end of the wage scale to go out to work to supplement family income. Indeed, there is some evidence that the pressure of low family income on women's participation is decreasing as all wages rise, though the issue is complicated by the declining ability of other family members to contribute to family income, a subject we have explored in the historical context. Still, that does not answer the basic question of why married women's participation rates are continuing to rise. Part of the answer lies in the fact that at least some of the increase is illusory.

The rapid rise in participation rates of married women in the postwar period coincides in part with the rapid decline in the importance of agriculture in the labour force. However, farm wives, though not usually counted as "in the labour force," are part of the family production unit. Increased urbanization, therefore, leads to the counting of women in the labour market who were not counted previously even if, in reality, they were part of the effective labour force. Monica Boyd, Margrit Eichler and John Hofley make the point that

> while in an agricultural setting the spouses were economically dependent on each other, the modern full-time housewife is economically dependent on her husband. As a result, her bargaining position vis-à-vis her husband has deteriorated. This loss is recouped, however, when she has an independent income.

In other words, there is a psychological pressure as well as an economic pressure on the wife to participate in order to regain her sense of self-worth.

The rise in real wage levels is also partly illusory. This is because of the way we count economic activity, a way that leads to an overestimate of the rise in real family income. The value of household production is not counted in a family's income, but if that household production is transferred to the market, it is counted. This includes everything from food preparation to babysitting, mending and washing clothes. At the same time the ability of family workers to contribute significantly to real family income through unpaid home work is decreasing. Where children were once considered an economic asset, the cost of raising children has now made them a financial liability. The Manitoba Department of Agriculture, *Family Resource Management Guide* for 1991 estimates the cost of raising a child to age eighteen at around $145,000. Other recent studies have put the costs of raising and educating children even higher, in the hundreds of thousands of dollars for each child when this includes a university education. While these estimates are based on professional families and are undoubtedly, therefore, on the high side, the basic point remains true. As more and more family work is absorbed by or transferred to the marketplace, measured income rises because we measure market activity — but at the cost of lost, unmeasured income in household production.

This is compounded by the fact that many social benefits (for example, Canada Pension Plan, dental and life insurance, supplemental medical insurance) are tied to participation in the labour market and that taxes must be paid in money. Whether or not the goods and services provided by the public sector are worth the taxes paid, there is no discretion or choice as to whether they are paid or not. This is particularly true of land and education taxes and, in those provinces that levy them, of medicare premiums.

Added to these direct pecuniary costs which considerably reduce the buying power of nominally increasing incomes, is the social pressure, heavily reinforced if not initiated by advertising, to increase consumption and to purchase new consumer durables; that is, to maintain consumption standards relative to rising community expectations. Given this combination of overestimated real income, rising pecuniary costs, and rising expectations, the economic pressure on wives to enter the labour market and contribute to money income has become enormous.

This whole discussion is predicated on the assumption that real incomes of the majority of workers have, in fact, continued to rise. This is not the case for the average worker, particularly after we account for the rise in base unemployment in the recessions of the early eighties and again in the early nineties; the rise in housing prices, and for the steady increase in taxation, particularly consumption based taxes such as the GST. In one study for Statistics Canada, Picot, Myles and Wannell also documented a major decline in wages for young, new entrants to the labour market of 30 per cent between 1977 and 1987. Similar, or even greater declines are being reported for long-time workers forced to find new employment by plant closures and restructuring. The Economic Council of Canada and Statistics Canada have reported no increase in individual real income between 1973 and 1990 and only a marginal increase in average family incomes as a result of increased female labour market participation. Given the massive increases in consumption and income taxes initiated by the Conservatives in the 1980s, average incomes can be concluded to have declined significantly. The threat looms of even more massive declines in real wages as a result of competition from low wage regions of the United States and Mexico as a consequence of the neo-conservative North America Free Trade Agreement. All of these factors have added to the need for wives to provide a second income in many, if not most, families.

The argument that household appliances and smaller families have made household work less demanding and fulfilling, while increased education makes labour market activity more lucrative and appealing, would seem to be only partially true. As noted previously, increased education does have a positive and strong effect on labour market participation. On the other hand, most studies indicate that, despite the introduction of a steady stream of improved household appliances, the time required for housework has not decreased much over the decades, though some of the physical drudgery may have been reduced. An American study, for instance, indicated that household work for a non-employed woman required about fifty-two hours per week in 1924 and fifty-five hours per week in 1968. This is almost exactly the same time requirement found in a Canadian study reported in 1981. Figures for Toronto in 1980 quoted by Gunderson, Muszynski and Keck for a five-day work week suggest that 36 hours of home work were typical for non-employed housewives. If women put in the same time on weekends as during the week, this would amount to 51 hours per week. Employed wives in these studies typically spent about half the amount of time or a little less on housework and child care, for the Toronto study 16 hours in a five day work week. Still, this represents a significant double burden on women workers, since these studies also indicate that most men do not significantly increase their household work to compensate for their wives' participation in the labour market. The Toronto study reported that men with wives in the labour market spent only one hour more per five-day week on housework for a total of 6.6 hours — but reduced their labour market work by over three hours. On the other hand, the 1983 study by Meg Luxton of wives in Flin Flon, Manitoba, indicated that at least some men were beginning to take more responsibility for work in the home, though with uncertain effects on the total time required of the women.

Perhaps the most important aspect of work in the home and the one most likely to deter women from participation in the work force is child rearing. The data from the labour force survey strongly supports this contention for all types of family status, particularly when the children were of preschool age (Table 2-4). This is not surprising given the record in Canada in the provision of day-care spaces. According to Connelly and MacDonald, in 1986 there were over 1.17 million children under six years of age of working mothers while day-care spaces reported in 1984 numbered only 172,000. This means that there were around seven children for every child-care space. The other approximately one million children of mothers working for pay were looked after by a combination of unpaid family members and paid babysitters. Nevertheless, participation rates have continued to rise quite rapidly, particularly for women with both preschool- and school-age children (Table 2-4). However, there is a significant decline in female participation as the number of children, both preschool- and school-age, increases. This is particularly marked for single parent families. For example, in 1986, the participation rate for lone parents with only one child was 56.2; with 4 or more children 44.1 (Connelly and MacDonald). Interestingly, however, the participation rates were higher for all women with two children than with only one.

The National Council of Welfare has estimated that in 1988 there were almost two million children of working parents who were under the age of 13 and required some form of day care. However, there were only sufficient licenced day-care spaces to accommodate 12.8

Table 2-4
Participation Rates of Women by Family Status and Age of Youngest Child, 1991

Participation Rate (%)

	Total, All Women	*With Employed Husband*	*With Non-employed Husband*	*With No Husband*
Total, All Women	61.3	73.6	30.3	56.3
With pre-school child(ren)	64.2	67.6	51.9	50.1
With school-age child(ren)	76.4	78.4	65.5	72.1
Without children under 16	54.1	74.2	23.4	49.2
Without children under 16, age under 55 years	79.3	81.7	64.6	78.4

(Note that the low participation rates of women without children is primarily a reflection of their age. This can be seen by comparing the last two rows, all women without children and women without children who were under age 55.)

Source: Statistics Canada, *The Labour Force, Annual Averages, 1991* (71-220).

per cent of these children. This suggests that despite the declining birth rate (26 per 1,000 population in 1961, 17 per 1,000 in 1971, 15 per 1,000 in 1981, and just marginally over 15 per 1,000 in 1991), the resulting decline in family size and the tendency for women to have their children closer together over a smaller age range have contributed to rising participation rates, this is only part of the answer and raises a further question: is participation rising because of falling fertility, or is fertility falling because of rising participation? Observers who stress the former explanation tend to argue that improved contraception bears major responsibility. However, the bulk of the information above, we believe, supports the second; that is, that increased participation in the labour market is one of the major contributing factors to falling fertility rates and smaller families. From the perspective of potential young parents, the difficulty and cost of raising a family, particularly a large family, lead them to postpone parenthood and have fewer children in order that the wives may work.

It would be useful here to elaborate on a number of factors that induce women into paid work. First, there are the economic pressures enumerated above, not least the rising costs of raising children —both the direct costs and the "opportunity costs" of foregone employment income. A second factor, more difficult to document, is the rate of family dissolution through widowhood, divorce and separation. But it is not only widows, divorcées and separated women who are affected. There have been numerous accounts in the media and in government and social-agency reports of the poverty problems encountered by single-parent, female-headed families that result from their failure to earn decent incomes; and by widows who fail to build up pension entitlement rights or who have had careers interrupted by family rearing. Thus, even for married women not as yet directly affected, the threat of such poverty is a strong inducement to enter and remain in the labour market as a form of insurance against the future quite apart from the independence and satisfaction the work itself may provide.

Finally, we cannot ignore the conventional economic argument that higher money wages, at least until the last decade or so, have made the "opportunity cost" of leisure and work in the home (the income lost in not going out to work) prohibitively high, pulling women into the labour market. This argument has been taken up by more radical economists, though with a different emphasis. Capitalist development, they contend, increases productivity in the industrial sectors serving the market through the mechanism of bringing a number of workers together in "cooperative organization" (with division of labour) and applying increasing amounts of capital equipment to the production process. The household, on the other hand, has remained backward, a backwater of low productivity due to minimal capital accumulation and individual production. One example frequently cited is the mass production of clothing which has made it cheaper to purchase ready-made clothes than to produce them in the home. This has been exacerbated in recent years by the expansion of free trade and lowered trade barriers that has allowed production of these household-competing goods to be manufactured in Third World countries at wages upon which Canadian women could not survive. Such being the case, it is only rational (in the sense that orthodox economists use that term) for women, if there is a choice, to enter into paid employment even though it means a double work load of paid and unpaid work.

The evidence, therefore, is that economic need, social and individual attitudes, and individual choice are all factors propelling women into the labour market from the early sixties to the early nineties at an accelerated pace. The stereotype of the housewife taking paid work as a temporary respite from the isolation and boredom of the household or to earn a little extra to purchase a car, some other appliance, or a family holiday, though it cannot be dismissed entirely, does not explain either the pervasiveness nor the magnitude of the movement of women, in particular married women, into the labour market. Were it not for a lot of unrecorded paid work in babysitting, house cleaning, home sewing and catering, the movement may indeed have been larger. The reasons, as we have argued, are much more fundamental and immediate. Regardless of these factors pushing women into the market, however, the movement could not have been sustained without a corresponding increase in employment opportunities for women.

The Demand for Women Workers

There is one overwhelming fact that has characterized the movement of women into the labour market. They have been employed in a very narrow range of occupations, a range that has changed negligibly throughout this century. The vast majority of women have been and continue to be employed in clerical, personal service and trade occupations, and in the teaching and nursing professions.

This is clearly evident in Table 2-5. What dominates this picture is the rise in, and continuing importance of, clerical work. Around one out of every three women workers in Canada is now employed in a clerical occupation. One out of every four in 1986 was employed in only five leading clerical occupations (four-digit Canadian Classification and Dictionary of Occupations code). This constitutes a ghettoization of women workers of formidable proportions, as illustrated in Table 2-6. Nevertheless, it has provided the opportunity for women to expand their market participation greatly up to the present time though, as the 1991 figures indicate, this may not be continuing in the face of the new electronic technology that has invaded the office and the retrenchment of public administration employment, a subject taken up in Chapter 5.

Part-time work is another factor that has allowed, perhaps even encouraged, some women to enter the labour market even when bearing a double burden of household work and child rearing.

Table 2-5
Distribution of the Female Labour Force by
Occupational Group, 1911-91
(%)

Occupational Group	1911	1931	1961a	1971	1980	1991
Professional	12.7	17.8	15.1	16.1	18.2b	21.3b
Clerical	9.4	17.7	28.8	30.5	33.9	29.1
Sales (Commercial and financial)	6.7	8.4	6.1	7.0	10.3	9.8
Service	37.2	33.9	22.4	17.4	18.5	17.1
Total	66.0	77.8	72.7	71.0	80.9	77.3

Sources: S. Ostry and M. Zaidi, *Labour Economics in Canada*; Manitoba Department of Labour, *Women in the Manitoba Labour Market*; Statistics Canada, *The Labour Force Annual Averages*, 1991 (71-220).
a There is a change in occupational classification in 1961. Under the earlier classification, the total figure would have been 76.9 rather than 72.7 per cent.
b Over 75 per cent of the professional group was made up of teachers and medical and health employees in 1980. By 1991, this had dropped marginally to just over 71 per cent.

Table 2-6
Women as a Percentage of Total Labour Force by
Occupational Group, 1901-91a

Occupational Group	1901	1931	1961	1971	1980	1991
Managerial	3.6	4.9	10.3	15.7	25.6	40.8
Professional	42.5	49.5	43.2	48.1	49.7	55.7b
Clerical	22.1	45.1	61.5	68.4	78.4	80.6
Sales/commercial	10.4	26.0	40.3	30.4	40.4	46.6
Services	68.7	62.1	50.0	46.2	54.4	56.7
Primary and blue collar	13.7	10.4	19.8	28.4	37.3	15.6
All occupations	13.4	17.0	27.3	34.3	40.0	45.0

Sources: Morley Gunderson, *"Work Patterns";* Manitoba
Department of Labour, *Women in the Manitoba Labour Market;*
Statistics Canada, *The Labour Force Annual Averages,*
1991 (71-220).
a Figures before 1971 are based on 1951 occupational classification,
after 1971 on the CCDO classification. Gunderson suggests that the
rise in the female percentage of managerial occupations from 1961
to 1971 and the corresponding drop in females sales percentage are
due in large measure to transferring of sales managers,
predominantly male, from managerial to sales classification.
b In teaching occupations, women constituted 64.9 % of the labour
force; in medicine and health, 80.3 %.

As Table 2-7 shows, in 1991 over a quarter (25.5 per cent) of all
women employees were working part-time, a rate that has held fairly
steady since the mid-eighties though up from 20.3 per cent in 1975.
(The comparable figures for male workers are 8.8 per cent in 1991
and 5.1 per cent in 1975). Moreover, over two-thirds of female
part-time workers are in the twenty-five years and older category
compared with under 40 per cent of male workers. (At that, the male
figure for older workers is inflated by the effects of the recession.)
That is, most male part-time workers are young, probably students,
working part-time to support their studies. In fact, half of male
part-time workers in 1991 were in school compared with less than a
quarter of the women. The majority of women, however, are older,
most likely wives supplementing family income or single parent

Table 2-7 Part-time Workers as a Percentage of All Workers			
Age and Sex	1975	1980	1991
Women			
15-24	22.1	27.2	43.4
25+	19.4	22.4	21.3
15+	20.3	23.8	25.5
Men			
15-24	17.1	19.4	35.2
25+	1.7	2.1	3.9
15+	5.1	6.0	8.8

Source: Manitoba Department of Labour, *Women in the Manitoba Labour Market: The Labour Force Annual Averages,* 1991 (71-220).

mothers attempting to juggle family responsibilities and avoid dependence on welfare.

Part-time work is not, in itself, a problem. Students and women with small children frequently seek such work. Problems arise, however, if people are forced to work part-time because full-time work is not available or if employers find it more profitable to employ several people part-time rather than a smaller number full-time and thus avoid paying fringe benefits such as pensions and insurance, or because it allows them to pay lower wages, since part-time workers are more frequently not covered by union contracts. Also, part-time workers seldom have access to job security or to promotion ladders. Over a quarter of women worked part-time because only part-time work was available while one half did so by choice and/or to accommodate family responsibilities. Involuntary part-time employment is a growing problem as neo-conservative restructuring of the economy (described in Chapter 5) takes place.

Thus, a limited range of occupational choice and a high percentage of part-time work are distinguishing characteristics of the expansion of female labour market opportunities, characteristics that have not proven conducive to economic equality for women and which do not bode well for their economic position in the future. The pervasive fact in this century is that more and more women have entered the labour market, but in a narrow range of occupations and at inferior pay to men. We will now turn to the question of the reasons for the inferior economic position of women.

3

Wages and Inequality

The advertising industry, having discovered the "new working woman," has increasingly portrayed her as affluent, powerful and upwardly mobile. While the overtly sexist advertisement of a decade ago, "You've come a long way, Baby," is undoubtedly true of cigarette consumption and the incidence of lung cancer in women, it is simply wrong if the true measure is earnings, income and career opportunities. In 1911 the average wage of employed women stood at 53 per cent of the average of male wages. In 1931 it was 60 per cent. By 1990 the average earned income of women who worked full-time the entire year was 67.6 per cent of men's full-year earnings, while the average earnings of all working women, including those working part-time or part-year, was still only 59.9 per cent of those of all men. The annual income of women was similarly only 59.4 per cent of male incomes, though this does constitute a significant gain of around 10 per cent over the previous decade (see Figure 3-1).

For every occupation group, for every age group, for part- and full-time workers, for every educational level and every region of Canada, men received higher average earnings. Although there has been some noticeable improvement in relative wages in the last two decades, it is slow and increasingly uncertain, and the dollar gap between men's and women's earnings has continued to grow. Table 3-1 gives a comparison of statistics on incomes and earnings that gives the dimensions of male/female differentials. Only one conclusion can be drawn from these figures. Over time, and across all characteristics, age, education, occupation and weeks worked, women still have a long way to go.

The question we want to pursue in this chapter is why women's relative economic position still lags so significantly despite twenty years of recognition that income inequality was a major problem. Perhaps the most frequently mentioned explanation is outright discrimination. Employers pay men more than women for the same jobs because they have a preference for male workers. Orthodox economists (admittedly mostly men) raise an important objection to this argument. According to them, if this were the case, then a smart employer would hire only lower-wage women, undercut the market, and drive the higher-priced competition out of existence. Only if there were a universal and all-inclusive conspiracy by employers to discriminate would women's wages be held consistently below men's. Though some feminists are prepared to argue this position, the history of attempts to regulate markets makes us skeptical of any explanation that relies on conspiracy to maintain market control, particularly across the economy and over long periods of time. This does not mean that discrimination does not exist, but rather that the basis of the discrimination lies in factors more complex than straightforward sexual preference.

Many observers who note the inferior economic position of women place the blame on women's labour market qualifications. Indeed, some go even further and suggest (as an advisor to former

Figure 3-1 Women's Earnings as a Percentage of Men's

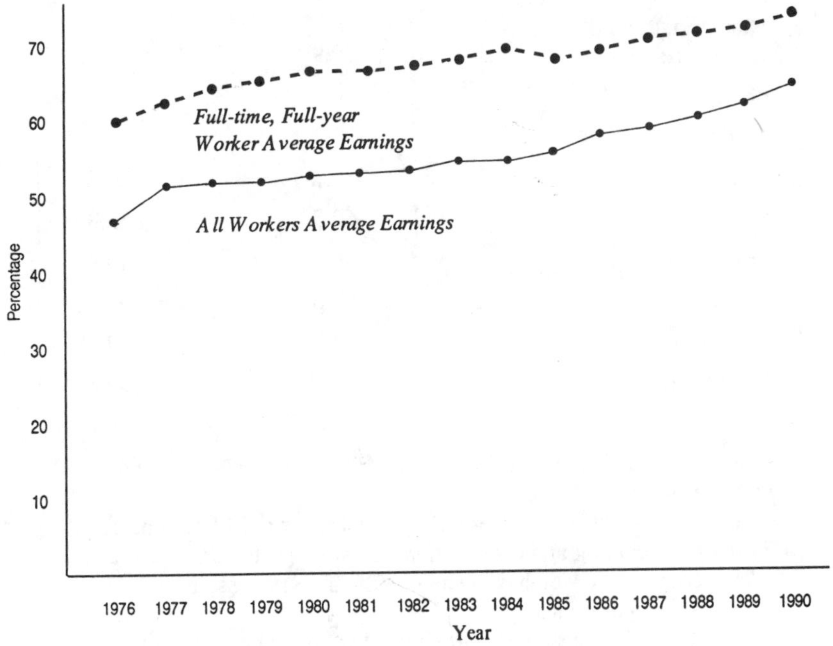

Source: Statistics Canada, *Earnings of Men and Women* (13217)

Table 3-1
Female Earnings as a Percentage of Male, 1990
(Full-time, Full-year Workers).

Age		Education	
15-24	79.0	0-8 years	62.4
25-34	73.8	Some high school	64.2
35-44	67.3	High school graduation	66.9
45-54	61.9	Some post-secondary	67.3
55+	64.3	Post-secondary certificate/diploma	67.5
All ages	67.6	University degree	72.8
Marital Status		*Work Activity**	
Single	89.8	Full-time, full-year	67.6
Married	62.6	All others (i.e. not full-time, full-year)	71.6
Other	74.8	Part-time, full-year	99.1
		Full-time, part-year	61.0
		Part-time, part-year	98.2

Selected Occupational Groups *Full-time, Full-Year*		All Workers
Managerial and Administrative	60.9	57.7
Profesional	70.9	63.3
Clerical	72.7	69.7
Sales	60.2	50.6
Service	60.5	55.3
Processing	58.6	49.9
Fabrication	60.6	57.1
Transport	60.7	49.2
Material Handling	70.5	70.5
Other Crafts	69.8	63.7

*full-year equals 49–52 weeks per year; full-time equals 30 or more hours per week.
**occupations where the sample is inadequate for reliable estimates (primary, machining and construction) are not reported. Professional is calculated from the weighted average of the five professional occupational sub-groups.
Source: Statistics Canada, *Earnings of Men and Women,* 1990 (13-217).

president Ronald Reagan did) that women are paid less because they are not willing to work as hard as men. This view represents the more extreme sexist version of this position. It is less easy, however, to dismiss the explanation that women, on average, have less education, training and work experience than men do and that this is reflected in relative wages.

Also more persuasive is the argument that women's wages are low because women are confined to low-wage occupations. This, of course, does not explain why women enter these occupations or why these occupations are poorly paid. Nevertheless, the concentration of women in a small number of relatively low-paid occupations is easily demonstrated. The relevant question is, why?

We have already established that the average woman's earnings and income are approximately 60 per cent of that of an average man. It is important now to establish whether this difference occurs because women are paid less for the same work — which is wage discrimination — or because women are shunted off into low-wage ghettos — which is job discrimination.

Wage Discrimination

The facts are that over the broad occupational classes, women make considerably less than men and that the differentials are not declining much over time. The figures speak for themselves (see Table 3-2).

The real question, however, is not as much in these broad occupation aggregates as it is in individual occupations. Here the evidence is neither quite so clear nor so dramatic. Table 3-3 gives ratios of earnings of a selection of more detailed occupations in Canada in 1985. These ratios indicate that wage discrimination on an individual occupation basis is considerably less than on the broader occupational aggregate basis. Even the earnings differentials demonstrated in Table 3-3 exaggerate the difference in wages by occupation in that women, on average, work fewer hours per week. The *Ontario Green Paper on Pay Equity*, released in 1985, estimated that over 40 per cent of the earnings differential of full time, full year workers in 1981 could be accounted for by differences in hours worked. A study for the Economic Council of Canada, based on data from the 1981 census, indicated that women worked only around three-quarters the number of hours that men worked and that strict adherence to the

Table 3-2

Women's Earnings as a Proportion of Men's by Selected Occupation Group: 1978 and 1990

Average Earnings of Full-time, Full-year Workers

	1978* %	1990 %	Absolute Difference 1990 ($)
Managerial and Administrative	54.4	60.9	19,007
Professional	61.7	70.9	13,101
Clerical	66.6	72.7	8,707
Sales	43.7	60.2	13,382
Service	48.1	60.5	11,410
Processing	53.5	58.6	13,808
Fabrication	52.0	60.6	13,355
Transport	66.9	60.7	13,336

* In 1978 processing includes machining; transport includes communications. Figures are for Full-year workers.
Source: Statistics Canada, *Earnings of Men and Women*, 1990 (13-217); Department of Labour, *Women in the Labour Force*, Pt. II, 1979.

principle of equal pay for equal work — that is, abolishing explicit wage discrimination — would improve women's relative incomes only marginally. Both this study and the *Ontario Green Paper* estimate that wage discrimination alone accounts for only four to five percentage points of the difference in male/female earnings. That means that eliminating simple wage discrimination would reduce the earnings differential of full-time, full-year workers by 15 per cent or less, in 1990 from 32.4 per cent to around 28 per cent.

The most frequent explanations for the remaining wage and earnings disparity are a combination of job discrimination — segregation of women into low-paying occupations — and a relative shortage among women of income-enhancing characteristics — education, training, work experience and unionization. (Unionization does tend to reduce wage disparities, a subject we take up in Chapter 6.) There is evidence to support the argument that this relative shortage is a significant factor in the earnings differential. Studies both in Canada and elsewhere that try to standardize for training and work experience suggest that about half the difference in earnings at the level of the broad occupational categories is accounted for by these two factors. The *Ontario Green Paper*'s estimate is somewhat lower, a quarter or less of the difference in full-time earnings. But whatever the actual figure, the conclusion of a 1979 study for the Economic Council of Canada remains:

> In short, full-time native-born paid employees who are women earn less than men because they do not benefit from the income relevant characteristics (education, training and experience) in the same manner as men.

Figures for professional workers with the same education and work experience bear this conclusion out. Even after standardization, women's earnings are less than men's though the differentials are considerably reduced, especially in those areas, such as teaching, that are highly unionized. Differentials between male and female teachers with similar experience reported in the late seventies were 4 per cent or less. *Canadian Social Trends* reported that in 1985-86 female principals' salaries were 96 per cent of those of male principals in elementary schools and 97 per cent in secondary schools, a marked reduction in inequality from a decade earlier. However, women were significantly underrepresented in these higher administrative ranks which partially accounts for the much higher differential in earnings at the broader occupational categories of elementary and secondary school teachers reported in Table 3-3.

However, the fact that women may have less training and experience can be attributed, at least in part, to a broader form of discrimination in schools and in society generally which tends to downplay women's career aspirations on the assumption that women will be forced to withdraw from the labour force for a significant period of time to act as home-maker, doing unpaid family work. Certainly, such withdrawal does have a very significant and direct effect in reducing continuous work experience. The evidence suggests that this has a major negative impact on women's earnings. Single women received 84 per cent of the earnings of single men in 1990, compared with 60 per cent for all women and all men. Also, women in the fifteen to twenty-four age bracket, most of whom will have had uninterrupted work experience, earned 87.6 per cent of male

Table 3-3

Female/Male Earnings by Occupation, 1985

(Average of Selected Occupations Employing Significant Numbers of Women)

Occupation Type	Number of Occupations	Wage Ratio as %
Clerical workers	21	77.7
Service workers	9	74.8
Sales	3	64.8
Manufacturing occupations, food	2	77.2
fabrication	5	71.0
Specific Occupations		
University teachers	1	74.9
Elementary school teachers	1	81.1
Secondary school teachers	1	87.2
Nurses	1	99.3
Nursing assistants	1	91.1
Nurse attendants	1	82.9

Source: Statistics Canada, *Census,* 1986

earnings. But by the thirty-five to forty-four age bracket, this ratio had fallen to 67.3 per cent. Although this is not conclusive evidence that disruption of work experience for family obligations is a major cause of low earnings, it is certainly supportive of this conclusion.

The bulk of the evidence, nevertheless, is that women receive significantly lower wages than men for the same type of jobs even when an adjustment is made for education and experience. On the other hand, there is also evidence that the earnings differential arises not just because they receive lower wages for the same or similar jobs but because women have been channelled into a number of low-wage job ghettos.

Job Discrimination

As pointed out previously, the majority of women enter a very few occupational categories, and these in general have income levels well below the average for all workers, male and female. Even for full-time full-year workers, clerical earnings, for example, were only 74 per cent of average earnings in 1985. Service incomes were similar, again 74 per cent on average, though women's wage and salary incomes in services were 55 per cent of men's. Average sales incomes for both male and female workers together were close to the average for all workers, but there is a major difference between males and females in this sector. Women's earnings in sales were less than two-thirds, women sales clerks' less than half the average level for all workers in all sectors, while male earnings were above average. What this suggests is that a significant component of the apparent wage discrimination against women is in occupational selection rather than outright wage discrimination.

Of course, this only tells part of the story. Within these broad categories are contained many specific occupations and women are disproportionately represented in the lower paid of these. It is significant that merely redistributing women among the broader occupational classes so as to match the occupational distribution of men would not in itself bring more income equality for women. The reason is that in the male-dominated broad occupational categories there is greater wage disparity between men and women than in female-dominated categories. As Morley Gunderson noted in 1976:

> Equalizing the occupational distribution would, to a large extent, transfer women from clerical and teaching occupations, where the earnings differential is small, to primary and blue-collar jobs, where the earnings gap is large.

What this means, on the other hand, is that if women received the same wages and hours as men, even if they remained in the same occupational sectors, as much as three-quarters of the earnings gap would be eliminated.

However, once one starts to break down these broad occupational categories into specific occupations, the picture begins to change. In a study of retail food store wages in Winnipeg, for instance, it was shown that in the larger, unionized firms there was little difference in the male and female wage for any particular occupation. However, checkout clerks, mostly women, had a lower wage rate than stock clerks, mostly men. Similarly, elementary school teachers, three-quarters of whom are women, received incomes in 1985 that were 4 per cent less than those of secondary school teachers, over 60 per cent of whom are men; and almost 30 per cent less than university teachers, over 80 per cent of whom are men. In the medical field, doctors, a male-dominated profession (83.4 per cent of full-year, full-time workers in 1985) receive incomes many times as high as the female-dominated profession of nursing. Cashiers and tellers, female-dominated occupations, received just 71 per cent of the wages and salaries of shipping and receiving clerks, mainly men; telephone operators, in majority women, again just 71 per cent of the employment income of the male-dominated occupation of mail carrier. In sales, men tend to dominate the "big ticket" fields like cars, real estate and appliances where commissions are substantial, while women are concentrated in low-price fields where commissions are small or non-existent. In fact, all of the ten highest paid occupations reported in the 1986 census were heavily male-dominated (Table 3-4). In contrast, of the ten lowest-paid specific occupations in the 1985 census (excluding the miscellaneous category of "other service workers," and "trapping and related" which accounted for only 155 people full-time, full-year; and lumping livestock and crop agricultural workers together as one occupation), eight were female-dominated representing almost six per cent of all full-time female employment. It is worth noting that the lowest paid occupation of all was child-care workers.

How can we explain this ghettoization of women not only in a small range of occupation areas but also in the low-wage jobs within these areas, where there is little apparent opportunity for promotion to higher-wage jobs? It is apparent from earnings data, for instance, that women's average earnings flatten out after they reach their mid- to late twenties while male earnings continue to increase for around ten years, until they reach their late thirties or early forties. We will explore some of the possible reasons given for both the ghettoization of women and low relative wages and job status of women.

Overcrowding and the Reserve Army

The overcrowding hypothesis argues that the supply of labour relative to demand has been much greater in female-dominated occupa-

Table 3-4

Ten Highest-Paid Occupations by Sex, 1985

(Full-Year, Full-Time Employment)

Occupation	Women as percentage of total employment	Female/male income ratio (%)
Physicians and surgeons	16.6	63.1
Judges and magistrates	13.8	77.9
Dentists	10.9	59.0
General managers	12.4	56.5
Lawyers and notaries	18.2	60.1
Air pilots, navigators and flight engineers	3.3	47.9
Osteopaths and chiropractors	10.9	60.8
Petroleum engineers	7.3	64.9
Optometrists	30.0	54.5
Management occupations, natural sciences and engineering	7.5	67.4
Top 10 occupations	13.3	60.2
All occupations	35.4	65.5

Source: Labour Canada, *Women in the Labour Force*, 1991

tions than in male-dominated occupations. As a result of the relative excess supply, wages in female occupations have been and remain lower by the force of competitive labour supply. This represents a form of discrimination which, as some have argued, originates in the preference of employers to hire either men or women for particular jobs even though there is no inherent differences between the sexes in potential productivity. As we have pointed out, however, this would require a general consensus among all employers to discriminate, and while this is not impossible, it is improbable and unlikely to account for such large differences in wage rates that it would pay employers to break with the consensus. On the other hand, it is probable that some unions, particularly in the skilled trades, have contributed to some occupational discrimination by restricting supply to prevent entry, not specifically of women, but of low-wage competition to high-wage occupations. We will return to this question later.

It would seem more logical, however, to look at the supply side of the market and the influence of general social attitudes and institutions. Stereotypes about what are appropriate jobs for men and women are ingrained early in life, reinforced by role models, the education system, counselling and by the societal expectation that women's primary commitment is to the household and reproduction function. This is confirmed by attitudinal studies of what most women themselves consider as appropriate female work. The effect of this social discrimination is to channel women into a narrow range of occupations, which not only keeps wages in these jobs low but also tends to undercut female wage levels in all other occupations even when they attempt to enter non-traditional jobs. This, in turn, creates the spectre of low-wage competition which encourages predominantly male unions to adopt policies of exclusion. As long as there remains a large reserve army of unemployed women in the household but available for work when the opportunity presents itself — or of underemployed women who work part-time or at low-level, low-wage jobs, yet who are capable of and willing to move into other, more productive areas — there will be considerable downward pressure on women's wages. The rapid rise over the last three decades in female participation rates is a graphic demonstration of the size of the reserve army and remains a formidable barrier to improvement in the economic position of women workers.

Much has been made recently of the progress of women into non-traditional job areas. This is particularly pronounced in the management area but, as the National Action Committee on the Status of Women has noted, these advances have been largely restricted to the lower levels, women supervising other women. In some other areas, such as engineering, the percentage increase of women has been quite significant. However, the initial representation of women was so small that the numbers themselves remain relatively insignificant. This is illustrated in Table 3-5 which shows the change in women's participation in some traditional male job sectors and specific occupations between the 1981 and 1986 census. In any case, it would take a massive change in women's participation in non-traditional work to have a significant impact in

Table 3-5

Growth of Female Participation in Some Traditional Male Occupations: 1980-1985

Occupation	Female Employment as % of Total, 1985 %	Growth in Female Employment, 1980-85 %
Professional		
Physical scientists	17.7	38.8
Architects, engineers, and community planners	7.4	62.5
Mathematicians, statisticians, and systems analysts	31.9	72.2
Forestry and logging	7.3	12.0
Mining and quarrying	2.1	-18.5
Machining	5.7	5.2
Mechanics	1.5	6.6
Construction trades	2.5	12.7
Locomotive operators*	2.2	10.3
Truck drivers	1.0	11.9
All occupations	43.5	9.7

* Not reliable due to low female sample
Source: Statistics Canada, *Census*, 1986.

"de-ghettoizing" the labour market. As Boulet and Lavallee note in their 1984 Economic Council study "even if every woman entering the labour force over the next 20 years were to choose a male occupation, the overall representation of women in these occupations would only reach 35 per cent at best."

What is the empirical support for the argument that the overcrowding of traditional female job markets by a "reserve army" of women is a contributing factor to the inequality in gender incomes? One piece of evidence is the higher rates of unemployment among

Table 3-6

Male and Female Unemployment Rates, 1966-1991
Average of Unadjusted Data

Year	Average Male Unemployment Rate	Average Female Unemployment Rate	Female- Male Differential
1966-70	4.3	4.4	+.1
1971-75	5.5	7.0	+1.5
1976-80	6.9	8.9	+2.0
1981-85	10.3	10.6	+.3
1986-90	8.1	8.9	+.8
1991	10.8	9.7	-1.1
1991 adjusted for involuntary part-time*	12.1	13.1	+1.0

*Estimated on the basis that the average involuntary part-time worker works 15 hours per week.

Source: Statistics Canada, *Historical Statistics of the Labour Force*, (71-201); *The Labour Force, Annual Averages*, 1991 (71-220).

women than among men — a rate differential that was in an upward trend until the recessions of 1981 and 1990 and free-trade restructuring devastated the male-dominated manufacturing sectors. Even despite these countervailing effects, over the business cycle female unemployment has remained significantly above that of males (Table 3-6). However, this is not the whole story. If we add to the officially unemployed the part-time workers who want to work full-time, then the female unemployment rate is much higher than the reported rates, by more than three percentage points in 1991 which would raise women's unemployment significantly above that of men's.

Further evidence is found in the occupational distribution of unemployment. Only in clerical and service occupations does female unemployment come close to male rates, though in both cases still higher. The occupations given in Table 3-7 are those with the highest percentage of women employees. Thus, it appears that there is a

Table 3-7

Male and Female Unemployment Rates by Selected Occupational Groups, 1991

Occupational	Male Unemployment Rate	Female Unemployment Rate	Female- Male Differential
Teaching	3.9	4.7	+0.8
Medicine and health	2.2	3.2	+1.0
Clerical	9.5	9.9	+0.4
Sales	7.1	10.3	+3.0
Service	11.8	12.0	+0.2
Processing	11.8	18.6	+6.8
Fabricating	11.5	18.5	+7.0

Source: Statistics Canada, *The Labour Force, Annual Averages*, 1991 (71-220).

reserve army of unemployed and underemployed among women. This does not include those women in the home, the latent pool, who might work if work were available.

Systemic and Statistical Discrimination

The predominant forms of discrimination in the labour market are not direct, specifically aimed at women because they are women, but because women lack, or are believed to lack, certain characteristics that employers seek. The most recognized form of this type is systemic discrimination, the setting of hiring standards or policies that exclude most members of specific groups such as women from employment in specific occupations or which relegates them to lower-pay job rungs even though those hiring standards or policies are not necessarily required for the job. Perhaps the classic case of this is weight and height requirements for police and fire fighters which while on the surface appear neutral, in fact have the effect of discriminating against women and members of ethnic groups that are characteristically small in stature.

Minimum education requirements unrelated to job requirements are another example, though of less discriminatory impact for women than for aboriginal and immigrant people.

More pervasive than systemic discrimination is statistical discrimination. Statistical discrimination occurs when employers resist hiring any specific group of workers — women, racial or ethnic minorities, young people — for a job or type of job because they *believe* that members of that group are more likely to have certain behavioural characteristics that reduce their long-term economic benefit to the employer. To be more specific, an employer may incur a considerable cost to hire and train a worker. In many firms, promotion and upgrading is done through experience and training on the job, not infrequently in situations involving expensive capital equipment. To minimize the cost and maximize the benefit, the employer will prefer to hire someone who can be expected to stay with the firm for an extended period of time and hence repay the training costs at all levels as the worker moves up the occupational ladder. Given the extensive capital equipment and the cooperative nature of production, it is equally important that employees be punctual, regular in attendance, and disciplined. Workers who are not believed to have these characteristics will be relegated to short-term, dead-end jobs that require either few specific skills or where the skills required are readily available as products of our public education system. Thus, if women are statistically more likely to quit a job or be absent from work, employers will tend to discriminate against all women regardless of their individual characteristics or patterns of behaviour and without regard to the societal causes of these statistical differences.

What is the evidence? This is set out in Table 3-8. Statistics would indicate that women voluntarily quit or leave the labour market or deliberately work part-time more frequently than do men, often as a consequence of family and personal reasons combined with the streaming of women into dead-end jobs. On the other hand, differences in absence from work due to illness are hardly very significant and almost certainly reflect the fact that when family members are sick, women are much more likely to be expected to stay home to act as nurse and report in sick themselves so as not to lose wages when sick leave is available or to deflect employer criticism that the family comes before work.

In most cases, women staying home when a family member is sick or quitting their jobs for family reasons or when their spouse is

Table 3-8
Measures of Work Stability and Regularity, 1991

Characteristics	Male	Female
Percentage of persons not in the labour force by reason of leaving last job		
Personal responsibilities	0.7	6.2
Illness	6.6	3.8
Percentage of persons unemployed by reason of leaving last job		
Personal responsibilities	1.2	7.2
Illness	2.9	5.0
Percentage of persons becoming unemployed by leaving (quitting) job	14.3	19.5
Percentage of persons working part-time by reason of working part-time		
Personal or family	0.1	13.1
Wanted to work part-time	17.4	36.3
Could only find part-time work	29.8	26.9
Percentage of persons working part-time	8.8	25.5
Loss of working time due to		
Illness	2.0	2.1
Personal responsibilities	3.9	17.5

Source: Statistics Canada, *The Labour Force, Annual Averages,* 1991 (71-220)

transferred or takes a new job in a different locality, is economically rational even where the couple maintains an equalitarian relationship. The reason is simple. Since most men earn more than their partners, the economic cost of women taking time off or quitting is less than if men do. This tends to perpetuate a rather vicious circle. In short, the statistics give some support, albeit hardly very significant, to the explanation that women's less stable work patterns are a basis for statistical discrimination.

This evidence and that in the previous section, however, are consistent with a third and different interpretation — that women have been channelled into low-income sectors for systemic reasons. They provide a disposable or interruptable supply of low-wage labour for marginal sectors of industry. But at the same time, women are kept dependent, meaning that they have few alternatives but to fulfil their role in the reproduction of the family and in providing unpaid home work, which reduces the cost of the provision of male workers.

It is not easy to marshal specific statistical evidence in support of this interpretation. However, there is historical evidence. As we noted in the first chapter, during the wheat boom period of Canadian development at the beginning of this century, federal ministers defended the refusal of the government to grant homesteads to women by the argument that homesteads would make women independent and thus give them alternatives to marriage, in which case men would be unable to develop their properties. The implication was that women were needed in the home as unpaid workers to guarantee the economic viability of the system.

Women and Poverty

Whatever the measure, whatever the cause, women do earn less than men. Their wages and salaries are less, women are disproportionately in low-wage occupations, and female unemployment rates have, in general, been higher except in recent years of recession with the decimation of manufacturing jobs. Some of the reasons have been touched on — lower training and work experience, statistical and other forms of discrimination, overcrowding — all of which have their roots in the sexual division of labour in the family, the historical evolution of the market, and the laws of motion of the contemporary capitalist economy in which discrimination plays an important functional role in making the system work. Before we turn to these broader questions, however, we should look at one of the human consequences, the poverty and degradation of a significant proportion of the population.

Poverty has been a growing fact facing Canadian women even as more and more women enter the paid labour force. Between 1971 and 1986 the number of women below the poverty line (Statistics Canada's "low income cut-offs") increased by 110.3 per cent, and women went from being 46 per cent of the poor in Canada to almost 60 per cent. One out of every six women in Canada lives in poverty.

Women may be in poverty for a number of reasons. For many, it will be the result of their own low incomes in the absence of a second income in the family. According to the National Council of Welfare in 1990, 84 per cent of women can expect to spend a significant part of their life without a husband or "significant other." Thirteen per cent of women never marry, and over a third of those who do marry will end up divorced or separated while 41 per cent will spend their older years in widowhood. Even if they are married and the spouse present, family income (one or other or both working) may still be below the poverty line, depending on wage levels, unemployment, and size of the family. The Advisory Council on the Status of Women study, *Women and Labour Market Poverty*, reported that in 1986, over half a million two-earner couple families, 9 per cent of all couple families, were below the poverty line. This represented just under a third of all poor women in Canada. Single women fared considerably worse. In the same year, 38.3 per cent were poor. Single-parent mothers present possibly the most visible case of poverty. In 1986, 44.1 per cent of female heads of single-parent families were impoverished even though a majority of them worked, at least part-time, and employment income comprised almost two-thirds of their total income. Single mothers working full-time had an incidence of poverty of 25.7 per cent. Those who worked only part-time had a poverty incidence rate of 75 per cent while those who were not employed at all and had young children had a rate in excess of 90 per cent. In all, single parent families constitute a third of all welfare recipients.

The characteristics of the poor family or individual are quite different from the popular stereotypes of the welfare bum. Almost half of all the poor people in Canada in 1986 worked for pay, approximately 30 per cent full-time. In fact, the incidence of poverty among working people has been growing faster than the other categories of poor. This is particularly evident among women. Between 1971 and 1986 the number of poor working women rose by 160 per cent, almost six times the rate of growth of poor working men. By 1986, 37 per cent of all poor women were working. Moreover, studies in Canada and the United States have found that very few, less than 20 per cent of welfare recipients, remain on the social assistance roles for any length of time. The vast majority do find work and, as their income situation improves, leave the welfare rolls. Nor does the stereotype of the family made poor by hordes of children have any basis in fact. Low-income families do not have significantly more children than do higher-income families. Single parent families had an average of 2.5 children in 1987 compared with husband-wife families with an average of 2.6. Although the probability of poverty rises with the number of children, it falls dramatically if the wife or single woman works, particularly full-time, regardless of the number or age of the children. A contributing factor, however, is that poor women have a lower participation rate than do non-poor women. However, more important, poor women are much more likely to be working part-time than the non-poor. The incidence of part-time work among the working poor was three times that among women generally. As Gunderson, Muszynski and Keck conclude, "this highlights the importance of part-time work as a determinant of working poverty, especially for women."

The problem of female-headed, single-parent families is particularly acute. In the first place, the incidence of single parent families has been increasing, a direct reflection of the rising rate of divorce and separation and the increase in the number of single women bearing and raising children. By 1986, single parent families represented 13 per cent of all families, 82 per cent female-headed. This is almost double the percentage of twenty years earlier. Table 3-9 illustrates the extent of this problem by age and in comparison with other groups of women.

Unattached women (living alone or with non-relatives) present a different, but major, situation. First, the incidence of unattached female households has also been rising, though not as quickly. A significant portion, perhaps a quarter, are young, many of them students and probably do not represent a significant poverty problem even though they may temporarily have low incomes. In fact, never-married, unattached women under 65 years of age have a high rate of labour market participation, 91 per cent in 1987, with 60 per cent working full time. The most serious situation is with older women, particularly widows. As the figures in the above table indicate, just under half (44 per cent) of unattached women over 65 have incomes under the poverty line. However, it should be noted that because of some recent changes in old age security provisions, this is a decline from about two-thirds a decade ago.

A great deal of female poverty is directly or indirectly related to women's inferior status in the labour market combined with social conditioning, sexual stereotyping, and their primary responsibility for the maintenance and reproduction of the household. Why are so many women poor? First, they are only about three-quarters as likely as men to participate in paid work and even when they do they are many times more likely to work part-time (and not be covered by a pension plan or other income security benefits), a consequence of the sexual division of labour that relegates women to unpaid work

Table 3-9

Poverty Rates of Women by Age and Status, 1987

Age	Poverty Incidence, Single Parent Mothers (%)*	Status	Poverty Incidence (%)
16-24	81	Never married single parent	75
25-34	69	Previously married single parent	52
35-44	45	Unattached, 65+	44
45+	33	Unattached, <65	33
All ages	57	Wives, children <18	10
		Other wives	7
		Wives >65	6

* A single parent mother is a single mother with dependent children.
Source: National Council of Welfare, *Women and Poverty Revisited*, 1990.

in the household. Second, when women do work they receive much lower wages than men, even for the same type of work. While the differences in male and female incomes among the working poor are proportionately less than in the general population, they are still substantial (Table 3-10). Social conditioning of women also tends to shunt them into a small number of low-wage job ghettos which, with some exceptions, lack job ladders or career paths. In 1986, for example, two-thirds of working women who were poor were concentrated in clerical, service and sales occupations. Most of these jobs, full-time and part-time, do not have private pension plans. In fact, women are, in general, much less likely to be covered by pensions. In 1987, for instance, only 38.7 per cent of women had employment pension coverage compared to 46 per cent of men, and even when they do have it, interrupted service for family rearing or the instability of their jobs or part-time employment reduces, or even eliminates, the possibility of women building up significant pension credits. In fact, of course, many pension plans simply are not port-

Table 3-10

**Male/Female Income Ratios, Poor and Non Poor
by Work Force Status, 1986**

Status	Women's Income as % of Men's
All individuals	55.3
Full-time working poor	77.9
Part-time working poor	79.3
Other poor	102.3

Source: Gunderson, Muszynski and Keck, *Women and Labour Market Poverty*, Table 3.9.

able. Even where service is continuous, full-time, and pension schemes exist, the lower-income levels of women mean lower pensions, particularly since women also tend to live longer than men.

The incidence of female poverty among older women makes the pension issue an extremely important one worth considering in greater detail. It is not only a question of labour market discrimination but also legal discrimination. Most pension plans, including the government's Canada Pension Plan (or its Quebec equivalent), are income-related, both in terms of the annual income earned and in the number of years worked. Women suffer on both accounts, particularly since pension earnings are compounded longer in the early employment years when women are most likely to be out of the labour market and are frequently based on the highest-earning years, which for career men are usually the last few years. For people without a career that involves upward mobility or who start careers late, pension earnings are necessarily lower even when they exist at all.

Far too many women, on the other hand, are forced to rely on their husband's pensions. But this security can be devastated by early widowhood or marriage breakdown. The Canada Pension Plan does make some provisions for marriage breakdown — CPP is supposed to be divided equally — but (except in Quebec where under the provisions of the Quebec Pension Plan it is done automatically) in only a very small percentage of cases does this in fact happen. For widows there is a survivor benefit but even with recent improvements, the maximum benefit, $334.75 per month in 1989, is obviously insufficient. Divorced women are not entitled to survivor benefits. Obviously, without legislation further improving both public and private pensions, the welfare of older women is indeed precarious.

Third, socialization, the education system and sexual stereotyping of certain types of work result in women getting less education or education in areas with much lower economic returns. For example, even at the university teacher level where salary differences between men and women are relatively small (an average of 5.2 per cent in 1988-9 when standardized for rank and professional degree), women are concentrated in those academic areas where wages, even male wages, tend to be lowest. They also tend to be in the lower ranks or have lesser degrees. This is illustrated in Table 3-11. Women are poorly represented in the four highest income teaching areas (except in health where over half were in nursing) and relatively better represented in the four lowest.

Table 3-11

Female Participation in University Teaching by Income Level of Teaching Area, 1988-1989

Teaching Area	Rank by Male Wage	% Female Instructors	Female/Male Wage Ratio
Engineering and applied sciences	1	2.9	71.8
Health professions and occupations (includes nursing)	2	24.8	78.3
Math and physical sciences	3	6.2	74.7
Agricultural and biological sciences (includes home economics)	4	17.3	79.9
Education	5	28.2	83.7
Humanities	6	23.2	79.7
Social sciences	7	18.2	80.6
Fine and applied arts	8	25.2	83.3
Not reported	9	28.3	86.4
All Areas		18.6	79.7

Source: Statistics Canada, *Teachers in Universities*, 1988-89 (81-241)

Table 3-12

Percentage of University Degrees, Diplomas and Certificates Granted to Women by Field and Level, 1990

Field	Percentage Female
Education	69.9
Fine arts	63.9
Humanities	62.8
Social sciences	53.9
Agricultural and biological sciences	54.0
Engineering and applied sciences	13.2,
Engineering	11.8
Health	70.0
Medicine	45.1
Nursing	95.4
Math and physical sciences	27.8
Not reported	63.1
Level	
Diplomas and certificates	62.4
Bachelor degrees	55.7
Master degrees	47.1
Doctorate degrees	32.1
Total, degrees, diplomas, certificates	55.3

Source: Statistics Canada, *Universities Enrollment and Degrees,* 1990 (81-204)

Even within these broad categories, women tend to be in the more poorly paid departments or disciplines or be in lower ranks. Thus, though the average wage difference when allowance is made for differences in rank and degree obtained is only 5.2 per cent, this rises to 20.3 per cent when not standardized.

Statistics for university and other post-secondary graduates give even more depressing evidence. This is readily evident in Tables 3-12 and 3-13. Although there has been some improvement in the last couple of decades in the sense that more women are entering non-traditional scientific and technical careers, progress is extremely slow while the concentration of women in the traditional professions of education and nursing remains distressingly high. Even within the social sciences, women are highly concentrated in two disciplines, sociology and psychology.

The same pattern can be illustrated with graduates of the community colleges. What is distressing is that after more than two decades

Table 3-13

Percentage Female Graduates of Community Colleges and Related Institutions by Program, 1989

Program	Percentage Female
Arts	58.7
Humanities and related	71.6
Health sciences and related	84.2
Nursing	90.4
Engineering and technology	16.0
Natural sciences and primary industries	32.3
Social sciences	74.4
Education	93.5
Business and commerce	65.7
Secretarial	98.7
Managerial and administration	56.7
Not elsewhere classified and not reported	60.7
All programs	58.1

Source: Statistics Canada, *Community Colleges and Related Institutions: Postsecondary Enrollment and Degrees*, 1989 (81-222)

of agitation by feminists, the educational channelling of women into traditional jobs that are not only lower paid but, with the exception of clerical work, are an extension into the market of household functions, continues virtually unabated. The implications for the income inequality and the incidence of female poverty remain.

Conclusion

We have tried to demonstrate in the last two chapters through the medium of the statistical record the fact of the inferior economic position of women in the labour market. In Chapter 1 we have also described some of the historical origins. Description, however, is no substitute for explanation. How did the inequality come about and why has it persisted into the present despite not inconsequential pressures by women's organizations and significant legislative enactments by governments to promote equality?

A number of possible explanations have been mentioned at various points in this survey of the historical and contemporary position of women at work. The range of opinion is wide. Some critics place the blame squarely on men for relegating women, whether intentionally or not, to a subordinate and dominated role in society. Many among the more radical economists are more likely to point the finger at employers and the owners of capital for exploiting the lack of bargaining power of women in the labour market and the competition among subgroups of the working people whether defined by sex, race, ethnicity or skill, for the pecuniary advantage of capital. Some sociologists look to social institutions as a cause of sexual stereotyping dating back to pre-industrial societies, indeed even to biological bonding patterns of anthropoid animals. More conservative analysts and orthodox economists are apt to place much of the blame on the victim herself for not behaving more like a man in terms of educational attainment, work aspirations or even willingness to work as hard as men, but even here opinions differ on the reasons for this alleged behaviour. This list is not exhaustive, nor an attempt to describe all of the analyses, but merely an outline of the range of interpretations.

A problem with all these explanations is that they tend to be partial, looking only at specific manifestations of a more general phenomenon. In our view, it is necessary to look at the origins and functions of inequality in our economic and social system generally.

4

The Economics of Market Dualism

As a rule, orthodox textbooks in labour economics don't provide much assistance in explaining the persistence of the low wages, job ghettos and blocked advancement that have characterized women's market work since the beginnings of capitalist development. We have already noted some of the limitations of traditional economic theory in understanding the persistence of inequality. Still, economists have been reluctant to admit to the possibility that discrimination may be profitable and not just an aberrant and irrational prejudice.

It follows from this and the normal economic assumption that workers are paid and are hired in proportion to their productivity that if wages and opportunities are significantly different between male and female workers, it reflects the fact that women's productivity on average is less than men's, or that women choose to enter those occupations where labour productivity is low, though real income may be considered higher due to congenial working conditions, lack of job stress, no travel, and little responsibility. This leads to the conclusion that women are their own worst enemies, an example of the blaming-the-victim syndrome.

However, not all economists accept this approach, in large measure because of the experience with attempts to improve the economic status of other disadvantaged economic groups in society, most notably with the blacks in the United States in the sixties. The "war on poverty" initiated under the Kennedy administration began with the orthodox economic assumptions and attempted to solve the persistent low incomes and high unemployment in the racial ghettos largely by education and training. Improve the potential productivity of these groups, it was argued, and their market disadvantage would be removed. What followed was a vast expansion in the educational and training systems, not only in the United States, but also in Canada as it emulated the American example.

Billions of dollars later, some researchers began to assess the results. Instead of untrained, uneducated, poor and unemployed blacks, the expenditure had produced a whole new population of trained, educated, poor and unemployed blacks. Perhaps the best characterization of the failure was the imaginative title of one assessment of the war on poverty — *The Great Training Robbery!* Incidentally, the same arguments are again being heard as a response to the unemployment and wage decreases initiated by global restructuring and free trade. However, in this instance the Canadian government has been cutting the monies for education and training, further undermining the credibility of the orthodox economic prescription.

The Segmented Labour Market

Out of the experience with the war on poverty there gradually emerged an alternative explanation of the inferior labour market position of racial and ethnic minorities and, most important for our study, of women. There are a number of variants of this explanation but they all share one common perception — the labour market is divided into segments with limited opportunity for upward mobility among the segments. The first developed version of segmented labour market theory was known as the *dual labour market* theory, which postulated that the labour market could be divided into two segments. At one end were jobs that paid relatively good wages, where employment was comparatively secure, working conditions reasonable, opportunities for advancement existed, and management was constrained by customs and rules. At the other end were jobs that paid poor wages, where employment was insecure, working conditions poor, opportunities for advancement minimal, and management frequently arbitrary. The former was designated the primary labour market, the latter the secondary labour market.

Furthermore, the primary and secondary labour markets had significant additional different characteristics. The primary was dominated by white males, many of them unionized. On the other hand, the secondary had a preponderance of racial and ethnic minorities, immigrants, young people, and women. Unionization, if it existed at all, was weak. Study after study in Canada and the United States documented this basic division but most of the early studies merely described the phenomenon without explaining it. What was not initially understood is why this division existed, how it developed and why it persisted.

In the two decades or so since these early studies there has been considerable refinement and elaboration of segmented labour market theory. One of the early refinements was the incorporation into the analysis of post-Keynesian explanations of unemployment and inflation and also some elements of more radical analyses. The simple "good job-bad job" dichotomy of the early dual analysts was also gradually refined with the identification of different types of labour markets in what was previously considered the single primary labour market. The lower or subordinate tier of the primary market was designated to include all the relatively well paid but generally semi-skilled blue collar workers; the upper or independent tier to designate the technical, supervisory and professional ranks. Somewhat later, some analysts also identified a skilled worker or craft tier with quite different dynamics from either the lower or upper tiers. Thus the "dual," or "split" as it was sometimes called, labour market analysis evolved into a more sophisticated segmented labour market model. Nevertheless, in attempting to develop the political economy of segmentation, its function and its origins, a certain dualism of economic structure keeps recurring. The starting point of our examination of the reality of the contemporary North American economy, therefore, is recognition of the readily apparent existence of two basic characteristics: one, the domination of a small number of large and very large corporations surrounded by a large number of very small companies; and two, the pattern of both cyclical and seasonal instability in employment and output.

As John Kenneth Galbraith pointed out in *The New Industrial State* more than three decades ago, large corporations require a high degree of stability in the demand for their products. The reason is that these firms are highly capital intensive — that is, their investment in buildings and machinery is very large, and secondly, their machinery and the workers who run them are highly specialized. With a large investment in highly specialized plants and workers and with additional high investments in product development and design, these firms cannot easily turn to producing other goods or services, and if they can't sell their output, profits suffer greatly. Even though they may be able to lay off workers, they can't unload the costs of unemployed capital onto unemployment insurance. One look at the automobile and steel companies and the airlines in Canada in the early nineties gives stark evidence of what happens to such firms in a situation of high fixed costs and depressed demand. Thus, the automobile companies produce only about half or less of their parts "in house" and contract out the rest. In British Columbia the forest product majors cut about half their own timber and contract out the remainder to small independents. A second strategy is to maintain alternative facilities which are considerably more labour-intensive that can be utilized to provide flexibility in levels of output without tying up expensive capital.

A special case of this pattern arises in seasonal industries. Highly specialized capital-intensive processes are rarely profitable for seasonal operation, since the investment would be unutilized for a portion of the year. As a result, firms tend to use labour-intensive production techniques, since labour is a variable factor — that is, it can be laid off without expense to the firm (though not without expense to the worker and to society) — while capital is not, unless it can be leased on a short-term basis. Where there are seasonal operations ancillary to a large-scale, capital-intensive operation, it frequently behooves the firm to subcontract all or part of the operation to small-scale "independent" or, in some cases, individual operators.

The flux in the system, therefore, requires a dualistic capital structure between the large-scale, specialized, capital-intensive firms mass producing for the mass market and the smaller-scale, less-specialized and labour-intensive supplementary firms producing on a smaller scale for the peak and niche markets. But the corollary of this is that the smaller firms use less specialized, more flexible, and more labour-intensive techniques, resulting in lower productivity and, therefore, less ability to pay wages comparable with the concentrated sector.

Although this pattern may predominate in much of goods production, it is much less applicable to services or to clerical work where large-scale mechanization is generally not feasible — except, perhaps, in some aspects of word and data processing. Therefore, work in these sectors tends to be labour intensive, and the use of specialized capital equipment much less frequent. It is estimated, for instance, that the average production worker has more than twelve times the amount of capital equipment to work with than does the clerical worker. In the large resource-based megaprojects the figure would be more like one hundred to five hundred times as much capital.

Nevertheless, some service and sales firms do have large and quite massive investments in buildings, inventory and advertising. Think of the major hotel, department store and supermarket chains. For them, capital expenditures are also highly specialized and dedicated, relatively inflexible to demand fluctuations by the time of the day, week or season. To be competitive they rely on "flexibility" of labour costs, depending on part-time or temporary labour and on subcontracting.

The consequence of this basic market division is that the worker in the capital-intensive production plant is not only very productive by virtue of the amount and the specialized nature of the equipment available to work with, but because the firms themselves are generally large enough to have a significant measure of market power such that, except in very severe recessions or depressions, they can set prices at production costs plus a profit markup. In contrast, the worker in the seasonal or small plants or in services usually has more limited productivity as a result of a small amount of less-specialized equipment and is much more likely to be employed by small, or even larger, competitive firms which lack market power and must accept a market price, in many cases one set by the more efficient large-scale operations.

There are, of course, exceptions to this general pattern. Some small specialty businesses may be considered highly productive not because of the physical capital used but because of the human capital, specialized skill or ability employed — everything from the professions (doctors, dentists, lawyers, architects), to the skilled crafts, even to the high-class restaurants where the chef's artistry is paramount. Nevertheless, the overall determinants of market productivity are three — the physical capital employed, the human capital employed, and the market power of the firm.

This description of the production structure needs to be related to the labour market. Segmented labour market theorists describe the labour market to correspond. The primary labour market is composed of three tiers. The upper, or independent, tier is composed of those workers who are "paid for what they know, not for what they do," — professional, technical and management workers. The knowledge that gives these people their relative independence, command of income and horizontal mobility is predominantly abstract, theoretical knowledge obtained through formal post-secondary institutional training. The craft, or middle, tier is composed of those skilled workers who have, to this point, escaped the deskilling effect of technology. The very nature of most maintenance work means that it cannot be subdivided and deskilled. In the smaller, specialized firms such as those in tool and die manufacture, job printing, repair shops and specialized electronics manufacture, flexibility and versatility as well as skills are required. Perhaps the best example is on-site construction. Because of the needed skills, which can only be obtained through a combination of formal training and work experience, wages tend to be relatively high. The boundaries of the labour market are established by the total number of firms that require the particular family of occupational skills, not by an individual employer, and this gives the craft worker horizontal mobility similar to that of the upper tier worker. The long-run threat to the position of these workers is technological change. In the short run, however, the problem is periodic unemployment due to cyclical and seasonal fluctuations. Given high wages and an earnings-related unemployment insurance scheme, however, much of the cost of these fluctuations can be passed on to consumers or to taxpayers.

In the lower tier of the primary sector, the characteristic worker is generally considered to be the work-skilled production worker, machine operator or machine tender. The stereotype would be the automobile assembly worker employed on a production line. The employee does not need the general skills of the crafts employee or the abstract knowledge of the professional-technical employee but requires specific, if limited, skills to perform the operation to which he or she is assigned. Training is normally "on-the-job" and proficiency is associated with experience gained through repetition. Because the production line or process is technologically a team concept and correct operation of expensive capital is necessary to avoid costly downtime or repairs, a premium is placed on regularity, punctuality and consistency, characteristics that when practised day after day become customary. Because training is mainly on-the-job and productivity associated with work experience, turnover and absenteeism are extremely expensive for this type of employer. Therefore, it is efficient for employers to pay premium wages, known as efficiency wages, to discourage such labour instability. Wages, benefits and advancement are handled through institutions such as unions, seniority systems, or customary differentials.

The primary strategy that management has practised toward this segment of the market has been to make use of internal labour markets — promotion up a job ladder within the firm — which give workers a large degree of job security, subject to seniority, and a chance at promotion, although normally the highest position a typical blue-collar worker can aspire to is that of foreman. Thus, job mobility is vertical rather than horizontal as in the craft and upper tiers. Here we can see the scientific-management technique of job subdivision. However, because of technical efficiency, capital intensity, and market power, these firms can afford to pay high or premium wages, and although vulnerable to fluctuations in aggregate demand in the economy due to their capital intensity and their requirement to maintain their work-skilled labour force, they can avoid much of the labour costs through the state's provision of unemployment insurance and, to the extent of their market power, they can raise prices in recessionary periods to retain target levels of profitability.

But these job ladders, tied to increasing wage rates and other benefits, can be expensive. Therefore, even those firms that have high productivity and market power attempt to restrict them to as few workers as possible. This they can do by the creation of labour-intensive plants utilizing unskilled workers to serve marginal or fluctuating demands, or by the creation of occupationally segregated ghettos where the requirements of job continuity, work experience or union pressures allow them to do so. Hence, large firms will, in periods of peak demand, establish a subsidiary, labour-intensive operation in a rural area. Perhaps, more frequently, the large firm will subcontract peak demand to a small contract shop. Many firms will subcontract out ancillary services such as janitorial or food services where work continuity is not important. In the case of occupational segregation, large firms will separate their office staff from their production staff both physically and in terms of systems of benefits, seniority and promotion, and union jurisdiction in order to tap the female labour market with its high supplies of labour and lower wage levels. Thus, even when women work for the big firms, their wages may be closer to those in the secondary labour market.

The secondary labour market marches to a quite different drummer than the primary market. The excess supply of labour, skilled and unskilled, combined with routine tasks that do not require significant on-the-job training, experience specific to the firm, or job security and high wages to combat turnover, labour unrest or unionization, means that it pays employers to hire in the secondary market where wages are low, where there are few internal promotion systems, and where labour is both easy to hire and easy to fire. Because of the low productivity and large supplies of labour, wages are not only low, but they appear to be determined largely by the level of minimum wages, welfare levels or some community-accepted minimum that is frequently related to some traditional non-wage or share-cropping pursuit such as agriculture or fishing. Workers in this sector are not protected by custom, union or scarcity of particular skills or knowledge, which intensifies the problem of arbitrary management and the potential for worker harassment, sexual and otherwise.

The obvious question that arises from this description of the dual (segmented) labour market is why the primary labour market is stocked mainly from the majority male labour force, and the secondary from minorities, women and youth. Most analysts of segmented labour markets point to statistical discrimination for the primary explanation. As we noted in the last chapter, statistical discrimination is directed at the disadvantaged in the labour market. Women, youths, and migrants from non-industrial societies are perceived by primary employers to have, on average, a weaker attachment to the wage labour force. For women, this is strongly reinforced by social attitudes. This means that they are more likely to leave employment — youth to continue education or to shop around for jobs; minorities because they are not acculturated to the discipline and regularity of industrial labour; and women because they periodically drop out of the labour force for family reasons, particularly the raising of children. Because primary employers believe these groups are less likely to participate in an uninterrupted, unbroken, disciplined manner, they discriminate against them in hiring for fear of losing their investment in on-the-job training. If members of these groups are hired and subsequently leave the labour force, even temporarily, they lose their rung on the job ladder and are relegated to begin again at the bottom.

Furthermore, it is argued, the characteristics of the secondary labour market provide little incentive for these groups to adopt more stable work patterns when employed in this sector. Jobs are unstable to begin with, but even where jobs are stable, wages are sufficiently low, conditions sufficiently bad, and prospects of advancement so limited that workers have little to gain from stable patterns of participation and therefore participate at their convenience rather than at the employer's. For some at the low end of the secondary market, periodic bouts of welfare (or unemployment insurance if they have accumulated sufficient entitlement) may be utilized to relieve the drudgery of work. Employers, in turn, adjust their patterns of work organization to accommodate turnover, absenteeism and other manifestations of instability with the result that productivity remains low and there is no incentive to improve the work environment. Thus, the job characteristics reinforce the work habits and work habits reinforce the job characteristics in an unending circle.

The dual labour market analysis went a long way to explaining the income and employment problems of the disadvantaged of urban America. Its subsequent elaboration and refinement to fit the contours of the dualistic structure of the modern economy has been a valuable tool in analysing the problems of all disadvantaged groups. But it still leaves unanswered many questions relating to women's work. How do we explain the origins of this employment dualism? Why has it persisted even as more and more women demonstrate a primary commitment to the labour force? Why has clerical work, even in the large corporations, failed to develop internal labour markets comparable to those among production workers?

The answers to these questions are not immediately self-evident. One must look at a number of factors: how job structures emerged, the nature of women's work in the home, the latent pool of partly employed and unemployed female workers, and the response of male workers to the evolution of industrial capitalism. It is only possible to do this through an historical perspective.

The Historical Roots of Labour Market Dualism

The historical sketch of women's work in Canada presented in Chapter 1 provides the material record upon which we can draw in order to attempt to understand the origins of contemporary labour market dualism and, in particular, the specific position of women. As we noted, until quite recently, the vast majority of the population were engaged in agricultural production and subsistence craft production for household consumption. Even when production was for the market, the household remained the primary unit of production, and within the household, the primary division of labour was based on sex. Men were the hunters, the commercial farmers, the weavers; women the gatherers, the producers of household consumption goods, the spinners.

What was the basis of the sexual division of labour under household production? Physical strength may have played a part but was probably not the most important factor. Rather, more fundamental was the women's role in reproduction, not only in the simple biological sense but in the broader sense of reproduction and nurturing of the family. In an era when large families were common as a primitive form of social security to ensure the economic viability of the family in case of illness, disability, old age or death of a parent, and as a supply of household labour, and in a time when infant and child mortality was high, women were frequently bearing or raising children for two decades or more through the potentially most productive years of their lives. Though it is common to assume that high birth rates were the result of primitive birth control methods, most recent research disputes this. High birth rates were a necessity for the production and reproduction of the family. Research has also tended to dispute the commonly held view that in earlier societies the household unit was the extended family, comprised of several generations and close relatives living together, with the older women minding the children, thereby providing relief for the mother from child care. As a consequence of high birth rates, therefore, women were restricted, to a greater or lesser extent, to work in and around the home.

The sexual division of labour centred on the reproduction of the family, however, should not be construed as being the same thing as the patriarchal or male-headed family in which women played a subordinate role, a conception which has become a conservative stereotype. The origins of patriarchy are still in dispute, although the practice of passing the most important economic asset of any pre-industrial society, land, through the male lineage was a powerful force in perpetuating it. As in post-industrial societies, property ownership played a dominant role in determining power relations.

The advent of industrial capitalism marks a fundamental break with the pattern of pre-industrial production. The family unit of production gradually gave way to capitalist production. The significant difference is not that production was for the market where previously it was for self-sufficiency as is so often assumed, but that the unit of production ceased to be the family unit and increasingly became the capitalist firm. In the early stages, in the heyday of the skilled craftsman or artisan and before the development of the large-scale factory, in Canada between approximately 1840 and 1880, it was the men who were most affected. The heavy drudgery of canal and railway building and the work in the timber industry was carried out primarily by the poor male immigrants from non-industrialized, famine-ridden Ireland, though on numerous occasions they were challenged for the work by the French Canadian habitant from the base of his semi-subsistence-level farm. Whatever the working conditions, however, if the contemporary descriptions of living conditions are a true picture many of the women must have led a dreadful existence of household toil. For the skilled industrial worker, however, conditions were relatively prosperous, since, as one observer has noted, in the early stages of the industrial revolution the knowledge and technology that permitted industrialization was contained in the minds and hands of the artisan.

The growth of the factory system changed all that. In fact it was women and children who bore much of the brunt of the second phase of industrialism, both directly and indirectly. The factory system was destructive of skills. The knowledge and techniques that were previously in the hands of the artisan were incorporated into machines, which in combination with large-scale production allowed for the breaking up of skilled jobs into an increasing number of simpler tasks where dexterity, work experience, and obedience were the main prerequisites.

It was frequently women and children who were drawn or pushed first into the factories. There are, no doubt, a number of reasons why this happened. One was that, at least in the textile industry in Britain, the first process to be converted to factory production was spinning, which traditionally had been women and children's work in the household division of labour. Secondly, it has also been suggested that the smaller fingers of women and children made them superior workers. Thirdly, the degradation of the skilled worker made it imperative that other members of the family work in industry in order to maintain a minimum standard of living. It has been suggested that women's wages were set at a level that when added to a man's would produce a family wage sufficient for reproduction of the family and the labour force. But of all the reasons, two stand out above all others in the historical record: women and children were cheaper and they were more obedient, thus less likely to struggle against the wages and working conditions of emerging industrial capitalism. Obviously these reasons are not totally unrelated.

Why were women's wages so much less than men's? We have already suggested the family wage argument, but the historical evidence points to several other factors. Women were less skilled, or at least less skilled in the occupations valued in the marketplace, for they readily practised for pay the skills that were learned and practised in the home. Perhaps most important, women were considered transitory workers (though "women's jobs" were not), for the most typical pattern was for women to enter the labour market in their teens, only to leave after a few years for marriage and family reproduction. At this point their work changed from full-time participation in the labour force to a mixture of income-producing work (boarders, household piecework, irregular work) and household subsistence production, all designed to make the family wage a living wage, a difficult task for the majority of the working class.

Women had few other opportunities, not only because of their function as mothers. The peculiar morality of Victorian patriarchal society decreed it to be so and decreed an inferior social and economic role for females. In this, the governing male elite was aided by reformers and by working-class men. Reformers accomplished this by their zeal in attempting to combat the evils of industrial capitalism by restricting and regulating women's participation in the factory system. Working-class men aided the process by their struggles against employers to prevent low-wage competition and to maintain control of the high-wage sectors in order that they could attain and retain a living wage.

Thus, women were not only paid less than men when in the same factories, but increasingly certain jobs were identified as women's work, most frequently those that were an extension into the market of their traditional work in the home. The question remains as to why women were willing to work under such wages and working conditions. Again, there is no simple answer. The necessity occasioned by poverty was perhaps the most pressing reason. Even the mildest form of protest would usually bring instant dismissal for the great majority unprotected by scarce skills and in a labour market deliberately oversupplied not only by women but also by migrants of both sexes. The economic consequences of job loss could be severe for the family. On the other hand, the influence of social attitudes had much the same effect. Within the patriarchal family, women were conditioned to subservience and submission, ideal characteristics for their function in the labour market.

We must still answer the question of why men, on average, were able to maintain a superior position in the face of the reserve army of unemployed or underemployed women and immigrants. Marx, observing the deskilling and routinization of industrial work in Britain in the mid-nineteenth century, had predicted that competition would reduce men, women and children to the same low level of subsistence. This, however, did not happen. At least part of the answer was that the workers fought back, and in response, employers adopted a strategy that can best be described as "divide and conquer."

That is, management increasingly structured the work process in such a way that groups of workers were separated into segmented markets which redirected worker conflict with employers to conflict among workers.

What was the basis of this segmentation? One division was at the heart of the scientific management movement that coincided with the emergence of big business at the end of the nineteenth century in North America. This was the separation of the conceptual or thinking part of work from the production worker — a major aspect of deskilling — which created, on the one hand, an elite group of managers, professionals and technical workers and, on the other, an increased mass of unskilled or work-skilled labour. It should be remembered that around the turn of the century the vast majority of clerical workers were men. In the emerging industrial firm, where the majority of workers were production workers, the limited ranks of white-collar staff were an integral part of management, very often the training ground for those destined to take over the top management positions. This separation of conceptual work from production together with the growth in firm size, however, created a need for a vast increase in clerical occupations, what are now called information workers. It was this process that was accompanied by the opening up of clerical occupations to women, but with a major new difference. Clerical workers were increasingly separated from management as the principles of scientific management were applied to the office as well as the shop floor. Conceptual work was retained by male managers while routinized clerical work — bookkeeping, typing, filing, telephone routing — was separated off for the new class of female worker.

The reasons for this segmentation are obvious. The rising proportion of clerical workers meant that there was intense competitive pressure to hire the cheapest workers available — in short, women. Though clerical work does require skills, they were easily taught skills, generally provided free of charge to the employer by the public school system. But from management's point of view, this segmentation had another great benefit. It removed the threat of male workers having access to information about the operations of the firm, which could lead to demands for participation in both the process and the spoils of management. Socially, women were considered not to have any pretense at management aspirations, and indeed, very few did have, conditioned as they were by their subsidiary role in the patriarchal family and society. Furthermore, clerical work suited the goals of the middle-class reformers and, indeed, of working-class men and women as well. It began to open up just as the factory reforms were contracting the opportunities for female industrial employment. It provided a segregated job ghetto for women, isolated from the immoral influences of working men that so perturbed the middle-class reformers, and it helped to restrict the low-wage competition faced by men in many emerging industrial markets.

The growth of the large industrial and sales corporations (big business or monopoly capitalism) also coincided with, indeed was dependent on, two major social changes: the growth in literacy, without which advertising could not be effective; and the growth in sales organization and mass retailing. This was the beginning of the heyday of daily newspapers, which were built on mass advertising and which, in turn, spurred on mass production and mass retailing. As a result, and for reasons similar to those regarding clerical workers, opportunities for female employment in sales expanded likewise, encouraged also by the fact that seasonal and daily fluctuations in sales could be accommodated by the fact that women, given their dual responsibilities of contributing to family income and working in the home to ensure the reproduction of the family, were willing to work part-time.

The growth of literacy and its corollary, public education, also created an enormous demand for school teachers. Because of the cost of the labour-intensive teaching profession there was intense pressure to employ the cheapest labour source available, women, but this was considered both socially and economically undesirable. It would put women in positions of authority over young men. It would also require women to acquire the conceptual and technical knowledge and skills jealously guarded by skilled male workers and by male management. The compromise was to restrict women teachers to elementary school with the responsibility of teaching only basic literacy and socialization — the latter including instilling the prevailing mores regarding the sexual division of labour and function.

The advent of these new female job ghettos does not mean that women were excluded from all industrial occupations, but the process of change was complex. On the production floor, the deskilling of craftsmen prompted an intense period of class conflict between employers and workers led initially by unions such as the Knights of Labor and increasingly after the 1880s by the craft unions. The result can best be described as a compromise. Some skilled workers were able to enforce an uneasy truce with employers that basically excluded the unskilled and which, given the sexual division of labour, also excluded women. Among the unskilled and deskilled workers, jobs were reduced to a structure of simple tasks, although many of them involved the need for work experience — that is, the knowledge and dexterity that comes from repeated operation of the same basic task.

What prevented workers from rebelling at this degradation of work? Indeed, employers were afraid of just such a workers' rebellion, particularly with the periodic rise of movements for industrial unions and of socialist doctrines from the 1880s on, culminating in the rise and final triumph of the Congress of Industrial Organizations (CIO) in the United States in the thirties and the Canadian Congress of Labour (CCL) in the forties. The threat of worker radicalization was known by the employers in the early years of this century as "the labour problem." Management strategies to deal with this problem ranged from direct, often violent, repression to the much more ingenious and, in the long run, more effective strategy of labour market segmentation, the creation of job ladders (which reduced insecurity and raised the possibility of improved wages and working conditions), the introduction of corporate welfare schemes (including profit sharing and pension plans) — all designed to create a loyalty to the firm, an interest in personal advancement and a reduction in class interests. Yet there still remained many jobs and industries that were not amenable to this structure, either because of the instability of the market or the inability to devise a technical process to replace the labour-intensive nature of production. These were the jobs and industries that continued to demand a low wage and interruptable labour supply. These were the jobs and industries that became the preserve of women and immigrant workers.

What is striking is the extent to which women continued to occupy the jobs that could be considered an extension of traditional household work — textiles and garments, food processing and other light manufacturing industries. In the heavy industries and the new manufacturing industries using capital-intensive, mass-production technology, metal works, later chemicals, appliances and transportation equipment, men predominated except in a limited number of light, labour-intensive assembly operations. Only in electronics where the technology continued to require labour-intensive assembly not unlike that in the garment industry (and therefore dependent on low wages), did women make significant employment inroads. These jobs became labelled women's jobs.

The growth of female employment in the service occupations is another graphic example of the transference of the household division of labour to the labour market. As we have noted, as late as the end of the nineteenth century the largest single employer of women was domestic service. Within a decade or so, domestic service was rapidly becoming an anachronism. The reason was the penetration of capitalist production into significant sectors of household work and the increasing availability of manufactured products previously fabricated in the home. Complementing this was the reluctance of women to enter personal service if any other employment opportunity was available.

The growth of female employment in services was merely a continuation of household work, only in the market — laundry workers, hotel maids, waitresses, charwomen, indeed even nursing and child-care workers. Whether in manufacturing or services, women's work remained women's work in the marketplace as in the home. The pattern established in this period of industrialization in North America has undergone little substantive change to date. As we have seen, average female wages have shown only limited improvement vis-à-vis male wages since before the First World War. Female employment is still concentrated in a small number of job ghettos, and although their relative importance has changed, the ghettos themselves have not — senior management, the engineering and technical professions, the skilled trades and all but light industry remain virtual male preserves. Women continue to fill the expanding areas of retail trade, clerical and financial low-level occupations; they still represent a high proportion of part-time workers and still lack extensive promotion or job ladders. In short, the dualistic structure "discovered" in the sixties and seventies and based in part on sex has its roots firmly planted in the rise of industrial capitalism, the replication in the labour market of the household division of labour, and the response of employers to the working class's struggle to oppose or at least to ameliorate the worst excess of industrial transformation and the rise of monopoly capitalism.

Yet despite the apparent continuity in women's roles in the labour market there has been the major change in the participation rates of women since the Second World War, as documented in Chapter 2. The forces propelling women into paid work and the changing structure of labour demand that has expanded employment opportunities for women have been in sufficient balance that relative wages have shown little movement. This tends to contradict some of the more romantic myths of the twentieth-century working woman. One such myth is that during the manpower shortage of the First World War women were liberated from traditional pursuits. Women did replace enlisted men in the factories, but even if they did acquire a taste for the material benefits of such work, few remained after the war. The myth was perpetuated through "Rosie the Riveter," the female industrial worker in the Second World War. In fact, unions and employers, even governments, tended to follow an exclusionist policy after the emergencies to restore jobs to men on the traditional grounds that men were the primary breadwinners. Particularly after the First World War, what women there were in industry generally returned to their pre-war pursuits, especially with the onslaught of depression in 1920. During the depressed thirties, efforts were made to replace women, where feasible, with men. In some cases, particularly in the public sector, married women were excluded by law from employment. Though the utilization of women in wartime production was more widespread during the Second World War, the occupational structure of the female labour force afterwards gives scant evidence of any social revolution in attitudes towards women in non-traditional work. The phenomenon was largely transitory.

Analysis of the record of the last century, therefore, indicates that the segmentation of the labour market that many economists found in the recent period has strong historic roots and has become an integral part of the contemporary economic structure. Class conflict that contributed to the creation of an institutionally segmented labour market guaranteed a measure of security and opportunity for advancement, insulating to some extent the primary labour market from competition. The opposite side of this coin, however, was the barriers to entry of women into this market, which made the secondary labour market bear the full force of competition from rising numbers of similar workers.

Women, Dualism and the Future

Women were not the only disadvantaged group to compete for low-level jobs, those jobs that the male, majority workers will not accept unless under duress because the wages and conditions have become so degraded by easy access to cheap, unskilled labour. In Europe there have been "guest workers" from the underdeveloped regions of southern Europe and northern Africa; in America, legal and illegal Hispanic immigrants; in Canada, natives, Asian immigrants, and migrants from the more depressed regions. These workers, along with the rising participation of women, have filled the less desirable jobs in the labour-intensive service, sales, manufacturing and agricultural industries and provided the labour supply flexibility that has allowed these areas to expand employment without placing excessive upward pressure on wage levels, which would have occurred in the absence of that steady increase in labour supply.

The growth in female participation has been particularly important given the growth in clerical work and in the public sector, the latter including the important health and education industries. Such an expansion would not have been feasible without a much more substantial increase in government expenditures and, therefore, in taxes, were it not for the latent reserve army of female labour. In this sense, the contemporary welfare state is in large measure built upon low-wage, female labour.

Nevertheless, if the primary labour market has been insulated to some degree from direct competition with reserves of female labour (and also by the tailoring of immigration policy to labour market conditions), there is increasing evidence that employers, particularly those facing world competition, are in the process of eroding the security and conditions of the primary market. This can be done through the use of women and other secondary workers as labour market reserves in subcontracting, part-time and irregular work, as well as through the automation of primary labour market jobs. But perhaps the most dramatic example since the early eighties has been the mobilization of the immense reserve army of unemployed and underemployed in the Third World through the agency of the multinational corporation and "free trade." Recent stagnation, falling real wages, and rising unemployment are reflections of this crisis. The danger is that this tactic will feed racism and sexism as high-wage workers attempt to protect their positions. As one observer has noted, employers do not create racism or sexism but they do exploit these pre-existing social divisions to their pecuniary advantage.

The feminist movement is challenging the caste system of female job ghettos and unequal pay through demands for equal opportunity (employment equity) and equal pay for work of equal value (pay equity). To date the record of success is not entirely encouraging nor is it entirely discouraging. The problem that must be faced is the threat women pose to higher-priced labour, a problem difficult to solve — and contemporary trends in the economy suggest it may become even more so in the future.

Michael Piore, one of the most prominent American economists developing the segmented labour market analysis, commented in the seventies about what he saw as the "tilt" of the economy toward the secondary labour market sector. What he meant was that technological change — mechanization, automation, robotics — was rapidly eroding the employment potential of the high-wage sector. In the resource area, job opportunities are indeed minimal and declining. In the manufacturing sector, as the automobile industry ably attests, the elimination of high-wage jobs is deemed imperative if North America is to compete with industries in low-wage countries or even in the higher-wage countries that themselves have adopted highly automated techniques and parts-sourcing from the Third World. Since Piore wrote many North American analysts have commented on the "disappearing middle," the decline in relatively well paid jobs, mainly in manufacturing (the lower and craft tiers of the primary labour market), the rise in high paid professional-technical work (the upper tier of the primary labour market), and the even more rapid expansion of low paid, unskilled work, particularly, but by no means exclusively, in services.

In their struggle to maintain their existing economic and social position, the male, majority workers will not be easy to convince that they should encourage the inclusion of large numbers of low-wage workers, including women, in the primary labour market in competition for a declining number of jobs. What is perhaps more likely are demands for increased security, which will effectively exclude people not now in the primary market from entry, thereby excluding them from the market generally or continuing to restrict them to low-wage job ghettos.

Technological change is not only a threat to the high-wage, male-dominated sector, however. As we will discuss in the next chapter, new technologies pose an equal or perhaps even greater threat to the reasonably secure and relatively better paid female job ghetto, clerical work. If the projections of the impact of electronic technology on information workers are near the mark, the eventual effect on this major area of traditionally women's work could be devastating, thus creating even more pressure on the high-wage workers to fight for exclusion.

Finally, we should recognize the rising problem created by the fiscal crisis of the state. Without attempting to describe the origins and causes of this crisis, we can note its symptoms — the inability (or unwillingness) of governments to maintain the levels of welfare state services without incurring massive and, to the business and financial sector, unacceptable budget deficits. Since it has been the public sector with its disproportionately high female employment that has provided the largest proportion of new jobs in the sixties and seventies, any further retrenchment in employment in the public sector will undermine good, existing female jobs and wage levels. This threat is exacerbated by another government retrenchment policy, the tightening up of unemployment insurance eligibility requirements and payments, which has a discriminatory impact on women because they are more apt to be employed in short-term, casual and part-time work. This has the further effect of undermining the community standard that underpins the wage level in the secondary labour market. To the extent that it does, secondary wages will be eroded, at least in relative terms, especially if women continue to be the majority (well over 80 per cent between 1980 and 1985) of new entrants into the labour market.

Conclusion

In order to comprehend the economic realities of labour market discrimination against females, it is necessary to understand both its function and its origins. Functionally, labour market segmentation serves a number of purposes. It provides a variable labour supply to accommodate the anarchy of the market while reducing the risks to capital; it divides labour into antagonistic groups based on pre-existing social divisions, which prevents the recognition of the common conflict of all labour with employers; it allows employers to divide up the market and pay the minimum necessary price for each group of workers (just as the airlines divide up the passenger market among business travellers, youth, families, pensioners, vacationers, so as to extract the maximum revenue from each group); and it provides the employer with the different sets of labour characteristics that are desired by different types and levels of operation.

The origin of this labour market segmentation lies in the transition from the household form of production, with its sexual division of labour which recognizes the woman's pivotal role in the reproduction of labour power and of the family, to the industrial capitalist form of production. Women as a group have never totally escaped from household production, either economically or socially. The result is the relegation of women to those unskilled (in the sense of marketable credentials) job ghettos that are a market extension of home production or, given the low productivity of home work, to the emerging labour-intensive occupations that rely on low wages, such as clerical work. The women's role in reproduction has also encouraged a broken pattern of labour market participation that has traditionally blocked access to job ladders. Nor can we ignore the adaptation of employers to the class struggle put up primarily by male workers in response to the degradation of work under industrial capitalism, which led to the capture of high-productivity, high-wage jobs for the primary male worker.

Understanding the function and origins of labour market segmentation provides no easy answer to its elimination. The problem is an integral part of the contemporary system. In Chapter 5 we will look at some of the current developments which threaten even the progress made to date. In Chapter 7 we will discuss some of the programs, achieved and proposed, designed to promote reform now and into the future.

5

Technology, Free Trade and Economic Restructuring: Women and the New Economic Order

It has become commonplace to describe the contemporary era as one of rapid and fundamental economic change, in the number and quality of goods and services we produce, and where and how we produce them. In the first edition of *Women and Work*, we concentrated on the microcomputer revolution that was raising new and formidable obstacles to the equality of women in the marketplace. A decade later it has become obvious that technological change is only one dimension of a profound economic and political restructuring that threatens to undermine the welfare of working people, both men and women. This restructuring puts into particular jeopardy the public programs designed to improve the relative economic position of women. New electronic, bio, and material technologies may be necessary to make this restructuring possible, but they are not sufficient in themselves to cause it.

What is also required is a revamping of the rules of the game. In the eighties, since the first edition of this book was published, such a revamping has taken place. The liberal socio-economic agenda that guided policy in the first three decades after the Second World War in North America and western Europe was replaced by what is now popularly known as the neo-conservative agenda — free trade and the "new global distribution of labour," deregulation and privatization, and retrenchment of government and of social benefits. The result generally has been a profound increase in income inequality, a rise in base unemployment, slow economic growth, and a progressive polarization of the labour market. As noted in the last chapter, restructuring and technological change has been eliminating jobs in the lower tier of the primary sector in favour of new jobs in the upper tier and, more significantly, in the low-wage secondary sector. While this process appears to be gender non-discriminatory in that "men's jobs" are even more jeopardized than "women's" (at least in manufacturing), in terms of opening up new opportunities for women its effect on the general labour market and on the potential for women to enter non-traditional blue-collar and skilled craft occupations is clearly negative.

While the various elements of the restructuring agenda are interrelated, it is perhaps easier to deal with their particular impacts on the labour market separately. There are three essential elements: technology, deregulation of markets and other economic activity (including free trade), and privatization of economic and social affairs (including retrenchment of the welfare state). Technological change, though not a cause of restructuring, is a necessary precondition.

Women and the Challenge of the Chip

Many people, perhaps most, are aware only as consumers of the new products made possible by the silicon chip — video games, pocket calculators, digital watches, car ignition systems, VCRs and compact disk players, the visual display terminals in banks, credit unions, and airline reservation offices, telecommunication and fax services, or perhaps, the home computer. On the surface, at least, we have come to terms with this new technology. But on much more important levels, we have not only not come to terms with it, we are barely even aware of the enormous challenge it poses — not to our consumption patterns but to production and employment.

The alteration of production made possible by the chip is revolutionary, comparable to the other great engineering breakthroughs such as the steam engine or the internal combustion engine. They changed the face of civilization — the way we live, the size and shape of cities, the supply of goods and services, and *the way we work*. With all the wonders and material benefits that they brought, they also brought misery, even starvation, to some. Technological change inevitably brings dislocations in production and employment. The important issue is how we deal with the problems created and how we utilize the technology. Historically, a common initial response has been to oppose the introduction of new technology. Early in the

Canadian industrial revolution when an employer introduced a sewing machine to his works, the tailors' union was sufficiently strong to have it returned to its supplier. The most famous example of this response was in Britain in the early nineteenth century: workers across the textile regions organized secretly under the banner of the mythical King Lud and smashed the frames and equipment of the masters.

Nevertheless, we must be careful to recognize that opposition to the introduction of new production technology has rarely been directed at the technology itself but rather at the unemployment and degradation of work, wages and working conditions threatened by the new technology. This is a major reason why, up until recently, automation and mechanization have largely been considered "male" issues. Women were not widely employed in the skilled crafts and therefore did not face the destruction of their skills. Most women who entered the factories in the industrialization period entered an already degraded workplace. The nature of most services and retail sales positions was such that personal contact and adaptation to individual needs made mechanization unfeasible.

In the growing clerical occupations, mechanization had limited scope. The demand for clerical workers was growing steadily as firms grew in size and sales and marketing became increasingly important, so job loss was not an important issue. Since new business machines as often as not reduced the drudgery of many office tasks, opposition to mechanization and automation in the office was muted. In fact, changes in much of the technology of the office were small, except perhaps in some areas of data processing. A typist before the First World War would find little difficulty in adjusting to most offices of the 1970s. The machinery would be recognizable and their functions similar though increasingly powered by electricity rather than by hand. The slowness of technical change is indicated by the fact that during the seventies productivity growth in the offices was only 4 per cent as compared with almost 100 per cent on the production floor.

The same cannot be said of mechanization in the workplace of many male workers. Mechanization meant that the tools ceased to be the extension of the skills of the individual and that the workers increasingly became machine operators, a transformation that permitted the employers to command increasing control over work and the worker and to employ lower-paid and less-skilled workers. Automation meant that the workers ceased to be machine operators and increasingly became machine tenders. While this transformation probably had less effect in degrading work other than increasing the element of boredom, it meant that many fewer workers were required. The spectre that haunted the worker, particularly in the sixties, was that of unemployment and/or of job loss, which would destroy the individual's rung on the job ladder, the source of the worker's security and his expectation of income progression.

The eighties turned that spectre into reality. Manufacturing and resource-processing, according to Heather Menzies in her study of technology, *Fast Forward and Out of Control,* are becoming "a subset of the information sector." By this she means that because of the revolution in information flows made possible by new electronic technology, the great manufacturing and resource firms are now able to produce wherever and whenever they have the advantage in labour, resources, taxes, energy, managerial or technical expertise. It is now much easier for them to restructure, outsource, shutdown and relocate, subcontract to low-wage regions or countries — encouraged by the spreading doctrine of free trade. This, of course, is in addition to the deskilling made possible by computer-controlled machinery and the direct replacement of workers with computer-controlled robots, electronic sensors and programmable tools. The result has been the "hollowing out" of the middle-income male working class and the polarization of the labour market that we have already referred to.

But perhaps for the first time, the spectre has also come to haunt women in a major way. Automation and robotization have now come to many of the deskilled but labour-intensive assembly and processing jobs that have traditionally been major employers of women such as the garment industry, fish packing and electronic assembly. For example, robots now do 85 per cent of the circuit-board assembly at Northern Telecom's Brampton plant. Sales work is also threatened by the spread of checkout laser scanners and universal product codes and, though still largely in the future, by home shopping by computer. Julie White in her 1985 study for Labour Canada, *Trouble in Store? The Impact of Microelectronics in the Retail Trade*, noted that jobs in trade in the decade 1966-1975 rose at a rate of 4 per cent per year but from 1976 to 1981 by only 2 per cent. In the following year jobs began to actually disappear, in 1981-82 by 36,000 or 2 per cent. However, the most threatened are clerical workers, and since they comprise almost a third of all women in the labour force, the magnitude of this threat looms large. The technology that makes this possible is the silicon chip but the motivation for its introduction is primarily economic — the profits of firms or the budget lines of public agencies.

The Bottom Line

Microelectronic technology developed at a propitious time for business. While production work has been steadily mechanized and automated since industrialization, office and clerical work has not, at least until quite recently. At the turn of the century, production workers comprised 90 per cent of the manufacturing labour force; by the eighties only three-quarters. (See Table 5-1 for 1988 figures.) By 1988, administrative salaries represented almost 14 per cent of the total value added in all manufacturing, and around a fifth in electrical and electronic manufacturing and in printing and publishing, both industries where women represent a third or more of their total employees. Office costs now run from around 50 per cent of total operating costs for major U.S. corporations, up to 75 per cent of costs for the financial industry, education and government. Wages account for 80 per cent of these office costs. What this amounts to is an enormous financial incentive for firms and for government to reduce office costs and the administrative wage bill. There are only two ways this can be done: reducing wages or increasing productivity.

In the past, cost pressures were not so great partly because of the availability of an elastic stream of low-paid female workers willing and, thanks to the public school system, able to staff the expanding offices. However, the growth of white-collar employment, which traditionally has been a fixed cost to firms (unlike blue-collar workers who can be laid off in periods of depressed business), the impracticality of attempting to lower wages significantly, and a small but nevertheless real threat of unionization have all placed pressure on business to automate the office. The goal is to produce the same amount of work with fewer workers, more work with the same number of workers, or the same or more work with cheaper (deskilled) workers. That is, the employer's goal is to increase the productivity of office workers by the replacement of labour or of skills with machines, as has been done progressively in production work. This is indicated by the fact that the average investment in equipment per worker in production is approximately twelve times

Table 5-1
Administrative Costs in Canadian Manufacturing:
Selected Industries, 1988

Industry	Administrative Employees		Administrative Salaries	
	% of Total Employees	*% Women*	*% of Total Wages & Salaries*	*% of Value Added*
All industries	24.3	32.5	31.5	13.6
Transportation equipment	21.7	37.6	26.5	12.1
Electrical and Electronic	31.0	29.8	40.8	18.5
Chemicals	46.0	35.4	52.1	13.8
Clothing	10.8	56.8	20.2	11.5
Food Processing	28.1	31.4	39.5	14.4
Printing and Publishing	37.7	50.4	41.5	21.3
Metal Fabricating	16.3	28.4	22.1	11.4

* Value Added is the difference between the value of the output of the industry and the cost of purchased materials, services, and intermediate inputs (i.e. it is composed of labour income, property income and profits).
Source: Statistics Canada, *Manufacturing Statistics of Canada*, 1988 *(31-203)*

the investment per worker in the office ($25,000 to $2,000 in the early eighties in Canada).

The barrier to replacing labour and skill with machinery has been the lack of an appropriate technology or, even after the introduction of the original mainframe computers, the extremely high cost of these machines that only a few, very large firms and governments could afford to install. Advancements in the technology, miniaturization and the development of mini- and microcomputers, however, have turned the economics upside down.

The Chip and its Uses

Prophetically, the origin of the word "computers" was in the name given to a group of 200 women hired by the U.S. Army during the Second World War to calculate tables of artillery trajectories. Because of the time involved for the women to do the calculations, the development of the first non-human electronic computer was begun in 1943 and completed in 1946. These early computers were enormous in size, filling rooms, and required large amounts of energy. The vacuum tubes were expensive to manufacture, large in size, unreliable, required energy for amplification, and needed an expensive temperature- and humidity-control system. Given these limitations, there was little scope for widespread use of computers. However, shortly afterwards the transistor was invented. It could do what the tubes did but was small, cheap and used little power. Essentially transistors were on-off switches that could be arranged in a pattern that gave the machine built-in computational logic.

Although transistors were small compared with tubes, computers were still very large machines and demanded the close environmental control of temperature and humidity. Military and space exploration demand for miniaturized computers, however, provided the impetus for further refinement. This was accomplished by the placing of more and more switches on a single piece of silicon until an entire circuit was constructed. Since this was first accomplished at the end of the fifties, the complexity of these circuits has increased by many hundreds of thousands of times, so that now the microprocessor or chip, the essential logic component of the computer, is smaller than a fingernail. Not only is it small, fast, and utilizes only microscopic amounts of energy, it is also inexpensive to produce in mass quantities. Moreover, the microprocessor can be designed for a wide variety of tasks and can be programmed to carry out different logical processes. The stage was set for the application of the computer to a wide variety of tasks of computation, of memory storage, and of instruction, including the ability to control other machines and monitor the results. It can also turn sounds and images into electronic bits of information that can be transmitted by line, microwave or satellite over vast distances and then reconstituted at the receiving end. Faxes and electronic mail are the most commonly experienced examples.

The computer, of course, cannot think. At least so far, artificial intelligence still eludes us. The thinking content of computers is installed in the design of the chip (the hardware) and the instructions given it by the computer programmer (the software). Once this capacity is installed, however, the computer is capable of complicated and refined tasks at very high speed. What is most significant, however, is that the intelligence required to perform much of the work is built into the machine by technical and scientific workers, while the operator of the machine need only know the rudimentary instructions to activate this intelligence. Thus, although the "hardware" has become cheap, the "software" remains expensive — except where the task to be performed is routinized and standardized packages can be purchased. In the organization of work, the implications are clear. Machine operators or tenders are deskilled, while conceptual and challenging work is concentrated in a small group of well-paid, technically trained workers and in the managers that control the designs of these systems.

The microprocessor can be utilized in a wide variety of processes that affect the workplace of both men and women. Women, however, must be concerned not only with the effects on what has traditionally been women's work but also with the effects on traditional male work. There are several reasons for such concern. The disappearance or degradation of skilled male work will severely limit the opportunities for women to break out of their occupational ghettos and enter non-traditional jobs. Secondly, male workers faced with diminishing job opportunities, particularly in the better-paid, skilled occupations, can be expected to attempt to monopolize the remaining openings and the higher-skilled, higher-paying jobs created by the new technology. In short, there is a danger that the impact of the new technology on male work will contribute to the crowding out of women from higher-order jobs in the future. Thirdly, the destruction of middle-income jobs threatens to destroy the entry ports and job ladders that are integral to entry into, and to the security and material benefits provided within, the primary labour market. For this reason, we will first review the potential impact of microelectronic technology on essentially blue-collar or production work.

The uses of the chip in conjunction with mechanical devices (robots) or with numerical-controlled, sensor-controlled or programmable machines, with information transmission, storage and retrieval equipment (data processing and electronic communications) or with automated materials-handling, testing and inventory management systems are virtually limitless. For the blue-collar worker involved in routinized assembly-line operations, the threat from robots and other computer-controlled machinery and tools has already been realized. The rapid decline in the cost of computers in the seventies and eighties means that the price of industrial robots has fallen drastically, in some cases well below the equivalent of an employee's yearly salary even in relatively low-wage sectors, although it may have a working life of up to ten years or more. Moreover, robots have none of the human frailties, can work faster, are readily retrainable — and never go on strike.

Nor is chip technology only applicable to mass production, low-skilled assembly work. Even small-batch manufacturing, engineering and drafting are affected. Rather than replacing the drudgery of production-line labour, however, these applications of the technology threaten the skills and jobs of occupations such as machinists and draftsmen. Computers aided by electronic sensors can economically operate metal-working equipment such as drills, lathes and milling equipment and are now readily programmable to accommodate short product or model lines. The skill of the machinist in converting blueprints to parts and in guiding the machine can be completely replaced, reducing the machinist to the status of a semiskilled machine tender. Computer-Aided Design-Computer Assisted Manufacture (CAD/CAM) allows an engineer to design products on a visual display terminal, transmit that design to a drafting machine and produce as many copies of the finished blueprint as are wanted. The draftsman becomes redundant.

What are the implications of this for women workers? As indicated above, women will be indirectly affected by the drying up of opportunities to enter better-paying non-traditional occupations. In addition, women employed in certain types of assembly occupations will be directly affected. Ironically perhaps, electronics and electrical assembly industries, where women represent approximately a third of production workers, have been one of the first industries hit. As already mentioned, in fish-packing, a female-dominated occupation, automatic gutting, filleting and packing machinery has seriously cut into seasonal employment. In the printing industry where women also comprise around a third of the workers, computers have had a major impact. Even in the garment industry where low wages and a flexible labour force might have been thought sufficient to protect the heavily female and immigrant workforce, automation has become quite pronounced, in the form of automated cutting and sewing machines and materials-handling systems. The potential for much more worker-replacing automation in the industry in the nineties is very great.

The Electronic Office and Shop

Far more directly significant for women are the applications of electronic technology to office work, to services, particularly in communications and finance, and to retail trade. These are the sectors that employ almost 60 per cent of all women workers and which absorbed almost half of all the increase in female employment between 1975 and 1991. The major applications of the computer and electronics in the office are in data and word processing and in communications, collectively referred to as information technology. The ubiquitous manifestation of this technology in the office is the visual display terminal or VDT.

The promise of this new technology is a dramatic rise in office productivity and the integration of information and decision-making within corporations, between corporations, regionally and internationally. A typist on a word processor can produce approximately twice the output that can be produced on a conventional typewriter through the virtual elimination of retyping, correcting errors and paper handling. In any office where customized variants of standard documents are produced, such as law and insurance offices, computers allow for instantaneous retrieval of selected text (sometimes referred to as "boilerplate") for inclusion in the document without the necessity of any typing. Similarly, with the integration of word and data processing and communications programs, composite documents complete with graphics can be produced and transmitted with minimal secretarial input. Filing and sorting, memo distribution, long-distance mail (through e-mail or facsimile transmission), can be done electronically . Computers can even correct spelling and grammatical errors.

The common attribute of this new technology is that it reduces the time necessary to do office work, if not immediately, then after the technology has become established in the office and integrated into network systems. The result can be manifested in one of a number of ways, most of which have negative implications for women. The most obvious result is a reduction in the number of clerical jobs, relatively and absolutely. Menzies, in *Fast Forward and Out* of

Control, reports on a Canadian Union of Public Employees (CUPE) survey in 1985 that showed a close correlation between the introduction of computers and job loss. Perhaps the best evidence is the relative decline in clerical work as an employer of women (34.3 per cent in 1981; 30.8 per cent in 1986; to 29.3 per cent in 1991); and, in the late eighties and early nineties, a fall in the absolute number of clerical jobs in the economy, (a drop of 1 per cent between 1989 and 1991). Studies in the United States of future employment growth also predict clerical employment falling relative to total employment in the nineties. In fact, one study by the eminent econometrician Wassily Leontief predicts a significant *decline* in the actual number of clerical workers by 1995 in the United States. A further measure of the decline in clerical job opportunities is the growth of clerical unemployment relative to total unemployment. In 1981 the rate of female unemployment in clerical occupations was 0.75 that of all female unemployment. By 1986 the ratio had risen to 0.83 and, by 1991, to 0.92.

Though increased unemployment of clerical workers is one manifestation, however, more important is "jobless economic and employment growth." By this is meant two things: though output has increased in the office, it is being produced by the same number of employees; and second, that office jobs are being widened to include new tasks without the creation of new jobs. Almost all studies report a marked intensification of work and increased work loads as a consequence of the introduction of computers into the office. However, what the CUPE and other studies have also found is that the most pervasive result of the introduction of the new technology has been the conversion of full-time and regular jobs to part-time, "temporary," or contracted-out work — with the obvious negative implications for women's income and career employment.

The expansion of part-time work at the expense of full-time jobs is the same result that has accompanied computerization of sales occupations, particularly cashiers. White notes that 56 per cent of sales jobs created between 1975 and 1982 were part-time, up from 37 per cent in the previous decade. Moreover, part-time hours are frequently reported to have been reduced. Stores are able to reduce the number of staff required to the minimum at any point in the day or the week through the information provided by computer monitoring and the flexibility provided by many part-timers all eager for more hours.

Other results widely reported are that the new technology frequently deskills, fragments and degrades clerical work and impedes career advancement. It deskills and degrades because it removes decision-making from the worker and imbeds it in the computer program, which is controlled by technical and management personnel removed from the main body of clerical workers. At the extreme, the word-processing or data-entry pools become little different from manufacturing assembly lines, both with repetitious and mind-destroying menial work — "Taylorism with a vengeance" as Menzies has characterized it referring to the deskilling strategy of F.W. Taylor, the late nineteenth century architect of "scientific management." Menzies, for instance, reports the impact on secretarial work in law offices.

> In the initial stage of stand-alone equipment, they organized clerical workers into word-processing pools where their typing was by rote and anonymous. It was classic scientific management, with work divided into standardized functions, and the execution or performance of it de-skilled accordingly. But as many standardized operations became automated, and when data- and word-processing were integrated, the work of document preparation was reorganized again. Standard word-processing is still done in the word-processing pool, often by a night shift employed on a part-time basis. Trained legal secretaries, on the other hand, have gained more scope and responsibility through the sophisticated software available to them.

This raises another consequence of the new technology. Certainly, there are cases of reskilling, the creation of new tasks that widen and deepen the responsibilities of some clerical workers. However, for the most part, the new conceptual and technical tasks are transferred up to senior managerial and technical staff, dominated by men, rather than down among the mainly female clerical workers. This has the effect of hollowing out job hierarchies. The deskilling of certain jobs and the upgrading of others widens the gap between the clerical occupations and the technical, administrative, professional and management occupations, which makes it increasingly difficult for clerical workers to gain access to higher-level jobs. Menzies, reporting on four case studies in an earlier book, *Women and the Chip* (1980) concluded that, not only did newly available upgraded jobs "move beyond the skills reach of the average clerical worker," but there was also a tendency toward increased isolation of female job ghettos "with few access points that would allow them at least a chance for upward mobility." Furthermore, deskilled work also encouraged part-time work —more barriers to career advancement, already impeded by employment stagnation and the ghettoization of clerical work and all contributing to the growing polarization of the labour market and of society.

The other common effect of office computerization reported in most studies, (and which clerical workers share with similar workers in telecommunications and sales), is the dehumanization and stress caused by electronic employee monitoring — how many keystrokes a typist makes in an hour or day, how many calls a telephone operator handles, how many sales a cashier transacts; how many times a worker goes to the washroom, how long she takes for coffee or lunch breaks — all become individually recordable for the purposes of managers who can remain anonymous. The intent of this is twofold, to increase the intensity of work for all employees and to identify, discipline or eliminate slower employees. This is reflected in the general response of workers that work loads increase with office automation and that the social and human character of the work is reduced. This, in turn, has led to the rise in stress-related illnesses among women subject to computer pacing and monitoring.

Perhaps one of the most reported recent cases was the "shocking" story of the Manitoba Telephone System. Telephone operators over an extended period of time reported problems with unexplained electrical shocks which eventually resulted in labour unrest and the shutting down of some facilities. Extensive testing was done of the facilities and equipment but without success in identifying the problem. Eventually, in consultation with the union, a new work organization was tested that reduced the stress level caused by close monitoring and routinization of the work and the problem seemed to largely disappear. This is not surprising. A statistical study by Julie Polle of illness and related medical and visual problems among clerical and telecommunications workers in Manitoba concluded that illness among these workers was unrelated to such things as the amount of time spent working at a computer or the physical (ergonomic) features of the work, but rather was directly related to the organization of the work — how little control the employee had of her work, the degree of monitoring, and the routinization and deskilling of the work. The question of the medical hazards from radiation emissions from VDTs, particularly for pregnant women, is still hotly debated (and as with asbestos, we may only find out the answer in cancer epidemiology studies twenty or thirty years down the line). For the moment, many union contracts do provide that pregnant women can refuse work at a VDT without penalty. However, even if it is eventually proved that emissions do not pose a threat, it is readily apparent that the stress produced by the electronic office does.

Stress and occupational health problems have also been some of the outcomes of the introduction of electronic checkout stations in supermarkets. White, for instance, reports on the back, shoulder elbow and hand problems that resulted from the "ring-and-bag" system introduced with electronic registers in the mid-1970s and on the decline in work satisfaction that accompanied the reduced interaction with customers demanded by the need to concentrate on continuous keying-in with electronic registers. Individual monitoring of the number of items checked through per minute is perhaps the most stressful effect of computerization, particularly in non-unionized stores where workers have no protection from discipline or discharge for not achieving manager-imposed norms.

The foregoing picture of the implications of the microelectronic revolution is hardly one to inspire great expectations on the part of women. However, it must be emphasized that few of these results are technologically determined. They are the result of how owners and managers choose to organize their work places. They are the result of how unregulated labour markets and traditional social attitudes discriminate against women, channelling them into low wage, dead-end job ghettos. Perhaps as well, the picture painted is too bleak. The new technology also opens up a host of exciting possibilities. Like the last industrial revolution, in the long run the new revolution may open up as many new jobs as it destroys. But that was scant comfort to the hand-loom weavers of nineteenth-century Britain, the harness makers of twentieth-century North America, or the women of early industrial Canada forced off the land and into the mills and urban squalor. It is also scant comfort to the office worker, bank teller or production-line worker made redundant by the micro-processor.

The challenge of the new technology is to the quantity and quality of jobs for both women and men. This, we repeat, is not determined by the technology but by how we choose to utilize that technology and by who has control over the terms and conditions of its introduction. The design and control of this new technology, however, is increasingly in the hands of private interests responding to the monetary rewards of an unregulated market and not to the social needs. The new set of neo-conservative rules, largely implemented during the decade of the 1980s, has created an environment that makes controlling the design and utilization of electronic technology in the interests of gender equality and quality of work life a much more difficult task.

Free Trade, Privatization and Women's Work

The 1980s, as we have noted, witnessed the emergence of a new political economy, an ideological policy agenda designed to achieve two goals, the deregulation of markets and the privatization of economic activity and decision making. The deregulation of markets included such things as the deregulation of the airline and trucking industries (with the consequent loss of many companies and thousands of jobs) but it is epitomized by the Canada-United States Free Trade Agreement (FTA) and the projected North American Free Trade Agreement (NAFTA). Despite their names, both agreements are more about deregulating and privatizing international markets for capital, technology and services than they are about reducing tariff and non-tariff barriers to trade. Nevertheless, the trade liberalization that is involved does have significant, and largely harmful, implications for the female labour market in Canada.

The privatization of economic activity and decision making, however, extends beyond the deregulation of markets. It also includes the sale of publicly owned enterprises, the transfer of public programs to the private sector, and the retrenchment of government services and cuts in public spending generally. Most of these actions also have a detrimental labour market impact for women.

The most comprehensive study of the impact of the FTA on women's work in Canada is *Free Trade and the Future of Women's Work* by Marjorie Cohen. The book was published some time before a North American free trade area was under active consideration, so it does not include an assessment of the potential impact of NAFTA. However, since NAFTA extends the same principles as contained in the FTA, the same effects on women can be expected though, perhaps, magnified. Cohen first looked at five manufacturing industries that account for over 60 per cent of women's manufacturing jobs: clothing, textiles, food processing, electrical and electronic products, and leather products. Her conclusion is worth quoting in full:

> [F]ree trade will increase women's unemployment, will confine women's work to an even more narrow range of occupations, and will adversely affect the ability of women to pursue better working conditions through unionization. It is also likely that the wage gap between males and females will grow and that competitive pressures will inhibit the effective use of social policies to correct the labour market inequalities between males and females.

The evidence in support of this conclusion is too lengthy to reproduce here in any detail, but the important factor contributing to the loss of these already low-wage jobs and to the inability to upgrade working conditions is competition from the low-wage, low-working-conditions standards and anti-union, "right-to-work" laws in the sunbelt (south and south-western) states in the United States and the Maquiladora corridor of Mexico.

Furthermore, women have a much more difficult problem adjusting to the unemployment caused by the "economic restructuring" initiated by free trade. They have more difficulty finding new jobs, remain unemployed longer and more frequently become "discouraged workers" and leave the labour force because they believe there is no work available to them. Even when they do find new jobs, many do so only at reduced wages (42 per cent in a 1980-82 Ontario study compared with only 25 per cent of men), at lowered wages relative to men's, and in traditional female occupational ghettos. They are usually less mobile, due to family ties, and are woefully underrepresented in training and retraining programs tied to the labour market.

Cohen goes on to analyze the impact of free trade in services. Her conclusions are generally similar, especially given the importance of services as a generator of employment for women. Particularly at risk are jobs in computer-related services and data processing. One estimate that she quotes puts the loss of Canadian jobs in data processing between 1977 and 1984 at 180,000 and this is forecast to increase markedly with free trade as multinational corporations concentrate their information services — and the "good jobs" that they represent — in their U.S. head offices. Already American employment per dollar of sales is almost twice that of Canadian employment per dollar of sales in major U.S. corporations with Canadian subsidiaries. Even more jobs are threatened by the deregulation of telecommunications and their potential centralization in the United States.

But the bigger threat to female workers Cohen sees is the pressure put on Canada by the FTA to "harmonize" its tax system, social services and public programs with those of the United States. This means a further retrenchment — more privatization, contracting out, part-time employment, cutbacks in social services — in a public sector already shrinking due to government measures to stem deficits and cut corporate taxes. The percentage of women employed in public administration has actually declined since the FTA came into effect, albeit marginally so far. The facts are that there is less wage and employment discrimination in the public sector and that education, health and social services are the largest employer of better paid female professional and technical employees of any industrial sector. In addition, existing employment and pay equity programs are, with the notable exception of Ontario, restricted to the public or quasi-public sector or to firms supplying the public sector. Therefore, any relative decline in public sector or related employment represents a further move away from equality with men. Furthermore, recent cuts in family allowance, unemployment insurance, and in the projected national day care program disproportionately affect women. Cohen concludes:

> The strength of the service sector is of vital importance to women workers in Canada since the majority of women are employed in this sector. Free trade in services will cause job loss and downward pressures on wages and working conditions in many areas which have traditionally been growth areas for women's employment: data processing, transportation, and public service occupations.

But the disappearance of jobs in the relatively non-discriminatory public sector is not the only threat to women posed by the neo-conservative attack on public services and social programs. Women have been the biggest losers in the recent cutbacks in unemployment insurance, particularly the abolition of benefits for those that "voluntarily" quit their jobs. This makes women workers particularly vulnerable to sexual harassment, since, if they are forced to quit in response, they stand to lose all future benefits unless they can prove the existence of such harassment, frequently a very difficult task. Moreover, women are more likely than men to quit their jobs to assume temporary family responsibilities. This imposes a double burden on such women — loss of employment and loss of unemployment benefits.

As already mentioned, one of the biggest blows to women from social program cutbacks was the abolition of family allowances, the only independent source of income many women were entitled to. It was particularly cruel for welfare mothers who faced having their provincial welfare allowances cut by provincial governments in order to "claw back" the amount of the previous family allowance that the federal government had converted into benefits for poor children. In the longer run, however, it is perhaps the reneging of the Mulroney government on its promise to introduce a national day-care program that will be the most costly to working women since, as we will demonstrate in Chapter 7, affordable, reliable day-care is essential to the equality of women in the labour market. Furthermore, all of these cutbacks tend to undermine the social wage that both supplements and supports wages in the secondary labour market already depressed by falling minimum real wages and rising unemployment. Again, as we have repeatedly demonstrated, this disproportionately affects and harms women in, and out of, the labour market.

Thus, free trade, market deregulation, privatization and public sector retrenchment combine with the new technology to present a daunting challenge to improving the status of women in the contemporary labour market. The question is, can this challenge be met and, if so, how?

6

Women and the Labour Movement

In the past, Canadian women have not been well represented among the ranks of organized labour. We will be exploring at some length in this chapter the historical, social and economic reasons for this low participation, but perhaps the first question that must be asked is, does it matter to their economic position that women are underrepresented in unions? The answer is that it does — if unions matter, if unions have a significant effect on wages, wage differentials, job security, fringe benefits, seniority and promotions, pensions and all the other terms of employment.

The consensus of most studies of the impact of unions on wages in Canada and the United States is that unions *do* matter. Although there is a fairly wide range in estimates of union–non-union differentials, the most common finding is that union wages average 10 to 25 per cent above non-union wages. However, interpreting these results is not easy. There is a disproportionate concentration of union organization in the large, capital-intensive, big business sector and in the government sector. Both sectors tend to pay higher wages than the smaller, competitive, labour-intensive firms, whether unionized or not. Furthermore, it can be argued that large non-union firms pay high wages to prevent unionization. On the other hand, among smaller, competitive firms or firms that must compete with imports from low-wage countries, unions have limited scope for raising wages before they "price themselves out of the market." Nevertheless, there is ample evidence to support the argument that unionization and the subsequent demands for higher wages force firms to become more efficient, to introduce productivity-increasing machinery and techniques, in order to survive. This evidence leads to the argument that unionized firms, by being forced to pay higher wages, mechanize and reorganize production so that they are able to pay higher wages. This argument is supported by the empirical evidence that unionized workers, on average, have higher productivity than do non-unionized workers. Whatever the cause-and-effect mechanism, however, a union member is likely to be paid more than a non-union member. This is demonstrated in Table 6.1 which sets out union wages as a percentage of non-union wages by status, selected industry and occupation.

What is indicated is that, with a few exceptions, women in Canada seem to benefit more from being unionized than do men (though this conclusion must be accepted with caution because all categories are a mix of different occupational levels, some unionized some not, where men and women are unequally represented). The categories where women do not benefit as much are concentrated in processing, fabrication and materials-handling occupations in manufacturing. This fact obviously reflects the industry mix: women are concentrated in these occupations in competitive industries (such as garments and textiles and food and beverage processing) where unionism probably has limited benefits for most workers, male or female. This fact may also explain why in the United States, where there is less unionization outside the manufacturing sector, women appear to benefit less than men. This table also shows that men are concentrated in the managerial and professional levels in both occupations and industries, above the status level covered by unions. We can see this concentration indicated in industries such as communications, public administration and finance, insurance and real estate, or in occupational groups such as medicine and managerial and administrative where the average non-union wage is higher than the union wage. Notice that this is not the case for women, which would suggest a higher concentration of women in the lower occupational ranks.

The impact of unions is not uniform. Some types of workers benefit more than others. Both Canadian and American studies generally suggest that unskilled, lower educated workers gain more from unionization than skilled, higher educated workers. A study of the Canadian 1974 wage structure by Wayne Simpson, published in 1985, showed that the union benefit of the lowest skilled workers was over 33 per cent but in the higher skilled levels it dwindled to 12 to 13 per cent and, in the highest of his seven skill categories it actually became negative. American studies indicate that blacks find it difficult to get into unionized sectors, but that when they do, they benefit more than whites. The evidence is pretty clear that whatever other effects unions have on wages, one overriding effect is to reduce wage dispersion and wage discrimination and, thereby, income inequality within the union sector.

Table 6-1
Average Wages of Unionized Workers as a Percentage of Non-union Workers, 1987: By Status, Selected Industry and Selected Occupational Group

By Status	Women	Men	Both Sexes
Total	136.2	112.8	121.9
Full-time	132.7	111.3	119.4
Part-time	158.6	167.8	160.5
By Selected Industry			
Manufacturing	108.3	95.5	103.5
Transportation	134.0	117.0	121.2
Communication	102.2	86.0	90.1
Trade	125.7	112.2	119.7
Finance, insurance and real estate	100.9	84.0	91.4
Community services	126.2	124.7	125.0
Business and personal services	107.6	93.9	103.1
Public administration	105.0	85.0	90.7
By Selected Occupation Group			
Managerial and administrative	109.1	98.7	101.8
Teaching	149.7	121.5	135.7
Medicine	116.7	80.5	107.9
Clerical	124.7	120.7	127.1
Sales	118.9	110.3	114.4
Service	164.5	148.9	166.5
Processing	128.8	114.2	120.1
Machining	154.7	122.2	124.8
Fabrication	119.7	125.2	127.2
Materials Handling	132.5	138.0	139.6

Source: Labour Canada, *Women in the Labour Force*, 1991

In her 1980 study *Women and Unions,* Julie White reported on male and female wages for both organized and unorganized office occupations. For the twenty occupations for which information was available for both sexes and both union statuses, the average differential between male and female wages was 10 per cent for unionized workers, 17 per cent for those non-unionized. Organized women received an average of 14 per cent more than unorganized women, organized men 8 per cent more than unorganized. Similarly, in their 1989 study *Gender Difference in Union Membership Status,* Pradeep Kumar and David Cowan conclude, "there is unambiguous empirical evidence that the earnings gap by gender tends to be smaller in unionized establishments than in non-unionized industries."

The problem is, however, that women are less likely to be unionized than men. As the previous table indicates, in some occupations and industries unionization is very effective in raising female wages; in others it seems to make little difference. The pattern, however, is suggestive. In the primary labour market, unionism tends to have particular benefit for the less skilled, for women and for minority workers. In the secondary labour market, however, unionism probably has limited benefits for most workers and is also less likely to exist in the first place. Since women are overrepresented in the secondary labour market, this will tend to limit the benefit some women may expect from unionism and to limit the number of female union members.

Wages, however, are not the only, perhaps not even the most important, benefit that accrues to the worker from unionization. Fringe benefits represent a significant part, perhaps near a quarter, of the workers' real employment income. According to Gunderson and Riddell's figures for 1978, the union to non-union wage differential was 30 per cent, the fringe benefit differential *75 per cent.* Since that time, in response to the recession and high unemployment and to a rising consciousness of women's special labour market needs, the labour movement has stressed fringe benefits even more, so this differential may have widened even further.

In addition, a collective agreement places a severe constraint on the arbitrary powers of management, particularly on the right to hire and fire, on disciplining, on fringe benefits, hours and overtime and, most important for many workers, on security and promotion up the job ladder without discrimination. Arbitrary management is replaced by rule by contractual agreement, greatly limiting the danger of a worker being victimized or discriminated against either for personal reasons or for reasons of race, ethnicity or gender.

It is true, of course, that unions themselves have not always lived up to the altruistic goal of non-discriminatory treatment implied above. Union contracts in Canada in the past have contained provisions for lower wage rates for women, Orientals and other minority groups. Some unions have deliberately tried to keep blacks and women out of certain occupations, particularly in the skilled building trades. But in general, the union maxim of strength in unity has encouraged a more even treatment of most workers within the organized sector. The fact that a large majority (70 per cent in 1989) of female workers are outside union ranks, therefore, is cause for some concern even though there has been a substantial increase in the percentage of women workers in unions over the last decade.

Traditional arguments for this low participation in unions include the following. First, women are antithetical to unionism because of their "petty bourgeois" attitudes within the individualistic family and because they are influenced by social attitudes towards working women, predominantly held by men. Second, related to this is the argument that women, because they periodically tend to move out of the labour force for family reasons and do not have the same career aspirations, see little benefit in unions while recognizing the costs of participation in organizing. Third, some suggest that female subordination to men originating in the patriarchal family is transferred to the employer, who is, with few exceptions, male and opposed to unionism.

Feminists are more prone to place the onus on men's attitudes, suggesting that traditional unions have not only ignored women's issues but have actively discriminated against women and have made little or no effort to organize them. They also tend to stress the dual work role of women, in the labour force and in the home, which leaves little time for such consuming activities as union organization and activities.

Whatever substance these arguments may have had in the past, there is little evidence that they are significant factors today, except perhaps in terms of women's participation in union executive positions. The overwhelming evidence points to the fact that women have a low level of unionization because the industries and the job ghettos they inhabit have proven difficult to organize, due to economic factors and the attitudes of their employers, not the attitudes of the women or the unions. This has been clearly demonstrated in several recent studies published by the Queen's University Industrial

Relations Centre. Pradeep Kumar, in a 1991 econometric study of union beliefs of Canadian workers, shows conclusively that gender has no influence on the likelihood of a worker being a union member once the independent effects of worker age, public or private sector employment, firm size, employment status and blue or white collar status are controlled for. Furthermore, gender had no influence on respondents' attitudes toward the necessity for unions. Indeed, in response to a question about the benefits of unions, women were significantly more favourable toward unions than were the male respondents. This tends to confirm the conclusion of Kumar and Cowan's earlier study that it is labour market segmentation, not gender, that is the primary determinant of union membership. "Controlling for age, marital status, education, nature of employment (part-time or full-time), job tenure and province of residence, the industry and occupation of employment account for more than four-fifths of the differential in the male-female unionization rate."

Furthermore, whatever its validity in the past, the feminist criticism that unions have tended to ignore women's issues in bargaining and in the political lobbying arena can no longer be maintained. This is one of the unmistakable conclusions of Julie White's 1990 study of the "consciousness raising" of the Canadian Union of Postal Workers (CUPW), Mail and Female, which traces the evolution of the union from one that opposed women workers, to one that is in the vanguard with respect to bargaining and campaigning for "women's issues." In 1962 only 4.9 per cent of the union's membership were women. By 1986 this had risen to 40.1 per cent. But this alone does not explain the rise of a feminist consciousness within the union. What began the process was the threat to male workers, and to the union, of the post office's increasing use of part-time workers, predominantly women, which the CUPW did not include in its ranks. By 1966, 20 per cent of postal workers were part-time, and with the Public Service Alliance and CUPE threatening to organize them, the Postal Workers reluctantly took them in. Somewhat to its surprise, they proved to be good and militant unionists. Attitudes began to change.

During the 1970s technological change in the form of the new postal code machinery was introduced. The majority of new hirees for the full-time coding positions were women who were paid 50 cents an hour less than the men who sorted mail manually, thereby creating "a predominantly female full-time occupational category, with a lower classification and lower rate of pay than the full-time occupational categories dominated by men." The union opposed this undercutting of the wages of all of its other workers. They also continued to oppose the expansion of part-time employees, an increasing number of whom were men, seeing in part-timers a source of cheap labour for the post office, again undercutting the wages of all the other workers. Thus the full-time/part-time division in the union began to cut across gender lines.

In 1981, the post office became a Crown corporation and the whole bargaining position was changed as CUPW now came under the Canada Labour Code, no longer under the Public Service Staff Relations Act. At the same time, the post office became more profit- and less service-oriented resulting in cutbacks and increased use of casual and part-time workers. But even before the post office became a Crown corporation and opened up new areas for negotiation, the union had broadened its bargaining mandate to include women's issues. As far back as 1977, the union had demanded paid maternity leave, but the turning point was the 1981 strike where it was among the union's main demands. Though not initially a central strike issue, maternity leave seized the public and media interest. Over the strong opposition of the post office and the federal Treasury Board, paid maternity leave was won, in part because of the public support for the union that the issue engendered. Solidarity, militancy, enlightened leadership — and a popular women's issue — had paid off for all the workers.

Since then, the bargaining agenda of items of particular importance to women has been broadened, continuing the theme of achieving an equality for male and female members which recognizes that men and women have different family responsibilities and that women may require special treatment in order to achieve equality. As a result, White reports that women members have recognized that the union has done a good job in protecting and furthering their interests — without women's committees, conferences or special female organizations within the union and despite underrepresentation of women in CUPW's executive ranks. This is not to say, of course, that there are no gender-related differences among the membership, particularly over issues such as sexual harassment, discrimination and access to the union hierarchy where men do not share the same problems. But in general, the union culture of struggle, of unified working-class consciousness, of working for the interests of all members, male and female, has paid off both for the union and for its female members.

The wider change in union attitudes generally is also demonstrated in a 1991 study by Pradeep Kumar and Lynn Acri, *Women's Issues and Collective Bargaining*, which shows clearly that women's issues have become "an integral part" of the Canadian labour movement's bargaining and lobbying agenda. Their conclusion is that the problem in achieving redress from discrimination is not the responsibility of the unions but of the employers.

The limited success of unions also reflects resistance on the part of employers to create an environment of equality in the workplace, apparently because for many years they have enjoyed a cheap source of labour at the expense of women.

Given a favourable economic environment, therefore, women have unionized and proven to be as dedicated and militant as men. Some male union organizers claim that women may be more reluctant to strike in the first instance but once on the picket line prove to be more tenacious and uncompromising than men. Perhaps this is also a stereotype, but nevertheless it tends to contravene a widely held perception. Other evidence comes from the history of women's involvement in Canadian unionism and the current structure of union membership.

Women and Unions: The Early Years

Prior to 1900, unionized women in Canada were few and far between. Only the Knights of Labor seems to have made any consistent effort to include women in its organization, although such organizations as the Knights of St. Crispin (shoemakers) did promote a Daughters of St. Crispin organization for women workers in the boot and shoe industry. This followed from the principle maintained by the Knights of Labor that to protect even the craft workers, all workers had to be unionized, and therefore they organized across national, sex and craft lines, skilled and unskilled. During the union's heyday in the 1880s, women joined the Knights, forming their own assemblies as well as joining in the men's, particularly in Ontario. One attraction for the women was the position held by the Knights of equal pay for equal work, regardless of sex.

However, as Ruth Frager has reported, "the male Knights were not as progressive as their rhetoric suggests.... Thus Leonora Barry, [the head] of the Knights' women's department, maintained that the 'selfishness' of the male Knights was partly to blame for the problems in organizing women." Still, there is other evidence that male workers did on occasion come to the defence of these early women unionists, such as in 1882 when male shoemakers in a Toronto union which later affiliated with the Knights of Labor went on a sympathy strike and provided material and moral support for their striking sisters, with the strong backing of other Toronto unionists.

One should not overemphasize the extent of female membership, however. Women were always a small minority and unionization was frequently transitory. Rather than unionizing, some women established benevolent societies, such as the Young Women's Christian Guild of Toronto, founded in 1886. These societies were not perceived as unions nor were they in fact. They were supposed to offer opportunities to young female workers for mutual improvement and social intercourse, as well as offer financial aid to their members in times of illness.

There are several reasons why women did not unionize more readily. To some degree the problems they encountered were the same as those met by men, but women experienced particular problems because of fragmentation of employment among many isolated workplaces. The royal commission of 1896 investigating the sweating system in Canada revealed that the greatest proportion of work was being done in homes, where factory laws were not applicable and where women had little contact with other workers. Fragmentation was also the norm for domestics, clerical, and shop workers presenting a formidable barrier to any organization attempt, while employers were frequently small and none too economically secure.

In addition, the Royal Commission on the Relations of Labour and Capital in 1889 gave evidence that organizing attempts by women were strenuously resisted by employers. When the Cropton Corset Company decided to start up a factory in Berlin (now Kitchener), Ontario, they took twenty or twenty-five expert women along to teach the beginners. One day while Cropton was away the women walked out as a group, demanding equal pay with the imported experts. The company responded by giving the women ten days to reconsider, and when they refused, the factory was shut down, an indication of how far employers would go to avoid giving in to women's organization.

Other industries employing significant numbers of women were also affected by organizations of their women workers. As Ferland has recounted, "the female weavers and spinners of the Hochelaga and St. Anne Mills (east of Montreal), and of Saint-Henri, Valley-field, and Cornwall, Ontario, got involved massively and openly in labour conflicts between 1880 and 1891," including the first-ever work stoppage in Quebec's cotton industry in 1880 — though once again the strike ended in failure.

Where women were working alongside men as a regular component of the work force, they would frequently have the opportunity to join the unions organized by men, though they were often not treated as equals within the union. But the evidence is that they were more vulnerable to employer intimidation. One cigar manufacturer testified that he preferred to hire women because they would not strike. This tendency of women to conform to the expectation of their employers is more understandable in light of later evidence that women joining the union were automatically fired. Whether the difficulties of organization were a consequence of their fragmented work situation or the opposition of the bosses, or even of the lukewarm support of male unionists and of a society generally that held to an ideology of domesticity, the net result was that few women were organized at the turn of the century.

However, with the exception of some of the skilled trades and the running trades on the railways, very few male workers were unionized as well. The initial burst of organization by the Knights in the emerging factories, spurred on by the National Policy Tariffs and the CPR construction boom, was petering out in the depression of the 1890s. Only the skilled workers, almost exclusively men, were able to withstand the dual forces of economic slack and employer opposition.

The factors that made unionization difficult for women in the nineteenth century were still present in the early years of the twentieth. Wayne Roberts in *Honest Womanhood* identifies several reasons why women did not organize as quickly or easily as men. Women were still scattered over many establishments and so did not have the contact with each other necessary to organize. They also entered the work force for a brief period, usually only for a few years, until they married. This high turnover of women meant that the experience and continuity necessary for organization was lacking, while at the same time it fuelled employers' opposition to employing women at equal pay to that of the more stable male workers. Even when they were in the work force, women changed jobs frequently because of boredom or dissatisfaction with degraded working conditions. When women did unionize, they lacked bargaining power, since with mechanization they had been shunted into unskilled work and, being easily replaced, were readily fired.

Despite these obstacles, women did make attempts to organize in various occupations. Although without a formal union, several small groups of sewing women struck in this period when piece rates were reduced, when immigrants were hired, or when they were fired for minor infractions of arbitrary management rules. Attempts from 1902 to 1904 to organize domestic servants, waitresses and clerical workers failed. Teachers were somewhat more successful in organizing though they never achieved a formal union. Roberts points out that although 90 per cent of teachers were women, the Ontario Educational Association had no women on its executive. Nevertheless, they were sufficiently organized and militant that in 1901, 500 teachers demonstrated at Toronto's city hall for a raise. Protests continued to be mounted in 1903, 1904, 1907, 1909 and 1910, and in 1910 they formed the Women Teachers Franchise Club.

In the printing shops women were somewhat more successful. Though working with men, they were not in direct competition for jobs. In 1901, 50 women formed the Women's Bindery Union in Toronto, which grew to 250 members within a month and to 350 by the following year. When the printers at Eaton's struck that year, the women could demonstrate their strength by walking out in sympathy. A similar situation existed with women telephone operators in Vancouver and New Westminster who formed an "auxiliary" in 1902 which, according to Elaine Bernard, was in fact a sub-local of Local 213 of the International Brotherhood of Electrical Workers. (It was not until 1911 that the union established a separate operator's — in effect a women's — department.) Within months both male and female members were out on strike, with the support of the other unions in and around Vancouver and Victoria. After a two-and-a-half-week strike both were successful, with the operators obtaining recognition, pay gains, sick leave and restrictions on the use of unpaid trainees. They were, however, not so fortunate four years later when the company was able to break the solidarity of the union and with it the operators' auxiliary after a prolonged strike.

One important point becomes clear. When women worked alongside men in the same industry, they frequently unionized with men. One example was the telegraph industry, one of the few skilled jobs in which women were significantly represented in the late nineteenth and early twentieth centuries, although women were systematically relegated to the less skilled, and thus lower paid, jobs within the industry. Another example of this was the Quebec textile industry. Forty per cent of the operatives in the cotton mills were women. The working conditions were difficult, with women often working in excess of sixty hours a week, a situation revealed when the mill workers struck in 1908 over wages and a reduction in hours. A royal commission resulting from the strike and headed by Mackenzie King uncovered the fact that the companies involved, the Dominion Textile Company and the Montreal Textile Company, had done their best to destroy any and all attempts at unionization.

The first attempt had come in 1899 by the American Federation of Labor (AFL), but was given up after a year. In 1905 the mule spinners tried to organize under the aegis of the National Trades and Labour Congress, but the local president was fired and the union fell through. In 1906 the United Federation of Textile Workers (UFTW) founded a local. When the company tried to break the union by getting employees to sign a contract guaranteeing they would not strike, 2,000 workers walked out. As a result of this show of solidarity, everyone was rehired, allowed to join the UFTW, and received a 12 to 14 per cent wage increase. For various reasons, including the problem French-speaking operatives found in an English union, the textile mill workers broke from the UFTW, forming the Federation of Textile Workers of Canada, which remained active from 1906 to the strike in 1908. Two-thirds of its members were women and they were among the most active members, an example of how women who worked in the same place as men, in the same industry, and under the same conditions, unionized much more quickly than other women.

Women, however, were not always the beneficiaries of existing male unions or of the organization attempts of men during the first two decades of this century. There are numerous indications of a general lack of commitment on the part of men to the cause of the organization of women. Within established unions the role of women was often portrayed as the wife of a union man, a reflection of the prevailing consensus of women's primary support role in the household. Female union members also usually received inferior settlements in wage disputes. When women tried independent union organization, as in the case of the Toronto Bell Telephone Operators, male organizers failed to extend the support necessary for the women to succeed.

It would appear from the attitude of many unions that the working woman was considered an anomaly — her role was as homemaker in support of her union husband. The important thing for a woman to do was to buy the union-label goods which benefited her husband, which in turn benefited her. Particular stress was given to the supportive role of the wife of the union organizer. Auxiliaries were formed to support union activities, particularly in strike situations when women were expected to support picketing activities. Whether it accurately reflected the male-to-female composition of the union or not, the union position indicated that men worked and women made the coffee. This attitude persisted well into the mid-twentieth century. As Sara Diamond has reported, however, the experience of women's auxiliaries was not always totally supportive of this male conception. "Women participants [in the IWA auxiliary in the 1930s and '40s], despite the emphasis on their domestic role, had begun to demand within their own homes an equal division of labour." Shortly after, the auxiliaries were dismantled.

When unions were consulted about the problems that women had, the men did not necessarily turn to working-class women for their ideas. Instead they often looked to spokespersons for the middle class. When a government investigation was made into the working conditions of women employed in shops and offices, the Vancouver Trades and Labour Council approached the Council of Women, a middle-class women's group. With this support a minimum wage was established at $5 a week, despite the fact that $10 a week was hardly considered an adequate subsistence wage.

In their agreements, unions also settled for lower wages for women than for men. In 1907 male bookbinders received from $13.50 to $14.50 per week, while women were only given $5 to $5.50 per week. This practice of settling for less money for women was common. A typical agreement in 1918 by the Hotel and Restaurant Employees' Union in B.C. provided a 50 cent per day increase for waiters while accepting a 17 cent per day increase for chambermaids. The settlement, which provided $22.50 a month for women, was estimated as half a living wage.

Male unionists were not particularly supportive of independent women's organizations. In several cases where women did organize independently of the men and sought support from the established unions, no support was forthcoming. This added to the women's difficulties. A classic example concerned the organized telephone operators in Toronto and Vancouver. Both groups appealed to the International Brotherhood of Electrical Workers (IBEW) for support, but to no avail. When the female operators went out on strike in 1906 in Vancouver, the IBEW, which represented the linemen as well as the women, quickly gave up paying strike pay. Though the local linemen remained supportive, the strike was lost, and the operators replaced.

In 1907 the same union followed with a similar failure. The operators for Bell Telephone in Toronto went out on strike. At issue was the company's decision to return to an eight-hour day schedule, after using a five-hour day schedule for several years, but without additional compensation or the payment of overtime. Again a royal commission was appointed. The hearings revealed that Bell Telephone was considering abolishing its two-week paid vacation and that working conditions were hazardous to the operators' health. The response of the women was to form the Telephone Operators, Supervisors and Monitors Association and to hire a lawyer to represent them. Bell's counter-offer was two pieces of paper to sign: a promise to work regularly and a resignation letter. Further than this, the company refused to negotiate. On 1 February 1907 the women replied with a strike. Public support rested with the strikers — a public strike fund was started, scabs harassed, and even the newspapers gave editorial support. The women considered affiliating with the IBEW, but the union failed even to respond. With the promise of the royal commission as incentive, the strike was called off and the women returned to work after a couple of days.

Unfortunately for the strikers, Bell did not feel bound by any of the conclusions of the commission. The inexperienced leadership and bad strategy that contributed to the failure of the strike might have been overcome, given the public sympathy with the operators, had the IBEW acted upon the initiative of the women and helped them through the strike. Not all male workers, however, turned their backs on the women. The bell boys refused to work in hotels where scabs were being housed during the strike, forcing the strikebreakers to find other accommodations. In another strike, involving women boot and shoe workers in 1912, men walked out in support. But in general there was a lack of concern by men for the interests of the working woman, even when they were organized in the same union.

Perhaps the most celebrated case of male abandonment came in 1919, at the time of the Winnipeg General Strike. In Vancouver the telephone operators were asked to join the sympathy strike, which they did. But when the general strike was ended, the operators refused to return to work until the issue of victimization of strikers was settled. The rest of the labour movement, however, failed to back them and their union was broken. In Bernard's words, the women were used as "'canon fodder' in a labour dispute in which they did not have a stake."

The advent of the First World War did bring some change with the opening up of non-traditional jobs for women. Despite the improved wartime labour market, however, labour's success at the bargaining table did not alter appreciably. In fact, employers used the war as an excuse to lengthen the working day and oppose strikes. The entry of lower-paid women who replaced the enlisted workers posed a real threat to the men. Labour's response to these new conditions brought a change in position. In 1898 the Trades and Labour Congress (TLC) had called for the removal of all women from the factories, mines and other industrial workplaces. Under wartime conditions, which meant loss of male workers through enlistment and eventually conscription, the Congress recognized that such a position was no longer tenable. Instead it adopted a demand for equal pay for men and women. The TLC realized that returning soldiers would be forced to take lower wages if employers were able to undercut the pre-war levels by paying low wages to women. As a result, through the war the TLC and the individual unions struggled to maintain good wages and hours for the women who worked in place of the men, but when the end of the war was in sight, the TLC started to work to have the women removed from their jobs to make room for the returning men. Women were only to be hired if there were no men to fill the jobs. Concern for the conditions of work for women during the war reflected a concern for the interests of the absent soldier, not for the factory "girl."

After the war and the wave of unrest that culminated in 1919 with the Winnipeg General Strike, depression set in. Not all the news was bad, however. Minimum wage legislation had begun to be enacted during the war to protect women from the more extreme forms of exploitation; though, in Winnipeg at least, the level of protection was less than half the "fair wage" level established by the federal government. The Amalgamated Clothing Workers in Ontario achieved an agreement that provided $20 for a forty-four-hour week with time and a half for overtime. This wage was still only 50 to 70 per cent of the prevailing male wage but was, nevertheless, an improvement over previous levels. However, the depression of the early twenties and the general retrenchment of all unionism during the decade meant little progress at the bargaining table for women or for men. Typical was the Federation of Textile Workers of Canada where women had been so active earlier in the century but which was now quiescent.

The Great Depression of the thirties hardly provided the conditions conducive to union organization. Yet workers did become more militant. Among women, activity was concentrated in the industries they had dominated, specifically the garment and textile industries. In Toronto and Montreal the International Ladies Garment Workers Union (ILGWU) and the Industrial Union of Needle Trades Workers competed to organize the women. The latter union led two unsuccessful strikes early in 1931 in Montreal. Meanwhile in Toronto the ILGWU led 500 out on a two-and-a-half-month strike, also unsuccessful. In 1934 it was the turn of the Industrial Union of Needle Trades Workers affiliated with the Communist-led Workers' Unity League. It struck in Toronto at the beginning of the summer but the main clash came at the end of the summer in Montreal. Faced with company opposition, police harassment, strikebreakers, Catholic anti-communism and inter-union factionalism, the strike failed. A measure of success finally came when the ILGWU led a strike in Montreal in 1937. The resulting agreement included a 10 per cent raise, a forty-four-hour week, and recognition of the union. However, once the employees returned to work the contract tended to be ignored by the employers. This lack of success was typical of the period, when women could be easily replaced. In some cases women did not have a chance to strike but were locked out as soon as they organized. Such was the practice of Eaton's, which locked out thirty-eight women when they organized a local of the ILGWU and demanded better rates.

The ILGWU success in 1937 was part of the growing wave of union organizing associated with the spread of the Congress of Industrial Organizations to Canada. Since these were industrial unions, those women on the shop floor were organized with the men. The other major industry affected where women were deeply involved was textiles. Under the leadership of the United Textile Workers of Canada they too struck in 1937, at Empire Cottons and Canadian Cottons in Ontario. It was in Quebec, however, that the biggest dispute broke out when Dominion Textile workers in seven plants struck. The union involved, the National Catholic Federation of Textile Workers, demanded a reduction in hours from sixty-four to forty per week and a raise in wages. Women's wages at the time were as low as $3.50 per week. The strike achieved an agreement that included a fifty-hour week and pay increases but no union recognition. Thus, despite the rise in militancy and support for unionization during the depression, the record of success for all workers, but especially for women workers, was rather bleak — even considering such important breakthroughs as the victory of the automobile workers at General Motors in Oshawa in 1937, despite the vigorous anti-CIO campaign of Ontario premier Mitch Hepburn. A better record required a stronger economy.

The Second World War brought prosperity to the Canadian economy as the demand grew for war supplies. Prosperity and a reduced labour force put unions in a stronger position to negotiate, including within those industries having a high proportion of women. The clothing industry in particular boomed with uniform contracts, and the Amalgamated Clothing Workers and the International Ladies Garment Workers were able to demand and receive union shop agreements. The United Garment Workers of America had lost members through the twenties and thirties but grew from 750 members to 12,000 by the end of the war. The ILGWU grew from 8,000 members in 1936 to 11,000 by 1948.

Despite gains in union membership and strength, all unions chafed under the restrictions of wartime labour legislation. In December 1940, Parliament limited wage settlements to the level of 1926-29 plus a cost-of-living bonus of $1.25 per week. Then in November 1941, raises in basic wages were prohibited and the National War Labour Board was given power to deny the bonus if they felt wages were already adequate. In 1943 the government made raises allowable only in cases of severe injustice and only if the employer could afford it. Nevertheless, one critical advance was achieved. In 1944, by Order-in-Council PC 1003, compulsory recognition of unions demonstrating support from the majority of workers in a plant was introduced. Pitched battles for union recognition would not be the barrier they had been in the past.

After the hostilities, workers tried to make up for the losses of the war. The textile industry was once again prominent in the struggle for better pay and lower hours. In 1946 in the Montreal area, the United Textile Workers of America, under a militant Canadian leadership, demanded an increase of twenty-five cents per hour, a forty-hour week, and union recognition, still not mandatory at the provincial level. The company ignored the demands, resulting in 6,000 millhands in Montreal and Valleyfield walking out. Montreal settled for a 6 cent to 11 cent raise and a forty-five-hour week, but in Valleyfield the issue became union recognition. The company had the organizers arrested and violence erupted, but certification was eventually won. In this case the union won but the majority of textile workers in the industry remained unrepresented. By the late forties only 40 per cent of the 75,000 textile workers in Canada were represented by a union.

Dominion Textile continued its anti-union fight, whereas the workers were divided by internal conflicts revolving around ideological and nationalistic issues as represented by several competing unions. In 1952 when the company instituted a speedup plan under the guise of a bonus incentive, the unions tried to fight it but they were bitterly divided between the National Catholic Federation of Textile Workers and the emerging Canadian Textile Council (at that time attempting to break away from the UTWA), each representing 6,000 workers. The company was aided by the anti-union reactionary administration of Premier Maurice Duplessis, whose career of strikebreaking became legendary.

In the late forties and the fifties, there was an effort to organize women outside the traditional industries of clothing and textiles. Attempts were made in professional, clerical and, most energetically, in sales occupations. The strikebreaking efforts of management, however, usually prevailed. One such unsuccessful attempt was to organize workers at the T. Eaton Company in Toronto. If the 15,000 employees had been organized as Local 1000 of the Retail, Wholesale and Department Store Union, the local would have been the largest in Canada. Under Eileen Tallman, workers were being signed up in 1948, but three years and a quarter of a million dollars later the attempt was abandoned. Eaton's had retaliated with a wage increase and pension plan. Combined with a high turnover of staff, organization proved impossible. The anatomy of this failure is chronicled in Eileen (Tallman) Sufrin's 1982 account, *The Eaton Drive*. It was neither the first nor the last union loss to this most intransigent, anti-union employer. In 1912, Eaton's locked out its unionized male tailors in Toronto. The factory garment workers, one-third women, walked out in support and were joined by Eaton's workers in other factories and in Montreal. Most of the workers involved were Jewish. Eaton's used native-Canadian ethnocentrism (anti-semitism) and middle-class feminist disdain for working-class women's issues to defeat the union boycott and break the strike. As Frager reports the "King of Canada" prevailed, the garment union was undermined, and for a long period "the T. Eaton Company would not hire any Jews." Eight decades later, as we recount below, the company prevailed again through exploiting gender and class, though in this case not racial, division.

Not all efforts were unsuccessful. In Montreal, Dupuis Frères had competed with larger stores, like Eaton's, through even poorer wages paid to widows, the disabled and the elderly. When prevailing wages in Montreal were $46.60 a week, Dupuis paid $30.00. In an attempt to win better conditions, the employees walked out on 1 May 1951. The company responded by opening the doors and offering a 20 per cent discount for self-serve. The tactic was not successful. By the end of July the workers had won an increase in wages, a forty-hour week, paid holidays, and union security.

Similar organizing attempts were made in the public sector, among government employees where women made up a large minority of the workers. The government proved no more amenable an employer. In 1959, 12,000 British Columbia provincial employees went out for higher wages but the issue quickly became one of the right of government employees to organize and to strike. The government resorted to the courts and labour injunctions to defeat the strike. Still, the evolution of public employee rights was under way. In 1964 the Bureau of Classification was established to sort out government pay scales, and a process of negotiation and arbitration was established. Saskatchewan civil servants had been granted bargaining rights by the Co-operative Commonwealth Federation (CCF) administration in 1944, but until Quebec made the move in 1965, provincial employees had made little further progress. The big advance came in 1967 when collective bargaining was introduced in the federal civil service a year after the two associations in the federal field had merged to form the Public Service Alliance of Canada (PSAC). By 1967 it was the third largest union in the country. In 1979 it was second in female membership only to the Canadian Union of Public Employees (CUPE), with almost 60,000 women members compared with almost 110,000 for CUPE, which organizes primarily at the municipal and hospital level. By 1980 the impact was substantial. Five out of the six largest unions in Canada represented public employees, a high percentage of them female health, education and clerical workers organized by CUPE and the National Union of Provincial Government Employees (NUPGE).

The leading role of public sector unions, however, has since begun to wane somewhat, a result of the concerted neo-conservative assault on public sector unions generally, in part because the public sector had ceased to grow and in many areas had begun to contract as privatization, contracting out and cutbacks in social programs took hold. By 1990 only three of the six largest unions in Canada were public sector unions. While the two largest remained CUPE and NUPGE, the Public Service Alliance had fallen to fifth. It also ranked fifth in 1989 in terms of female membership (Table 6-2). However, if the membership of the provincial nurses unions and provincial teachers unions were combined in a national organization, both unions would rank in the top four by female membership and in the top five or six in total membership.

What is also interesting is the rise in prominence in the last decade of two service and clerical unions with large female memberships, the United Food and Commercial Workers (47 per cent female membership) and the Service Employees International Union (71 per

Table 6-2	
Leading Unions by Female Membership, 1989	
Union	*Membership*
Canadian Union of Public Employees (CUPE)	197,914
National Union of Provincial Government Employees (NUPGE)	140,000+ (est.)* (67,834)**
United Food and Commercial Workers	86,122
Quebec Teaching Congress (CEQ)	80,686
Public Service Alliance of Canada (PSAC)	68,032
Social Affairs Federation (CNTU)	67,034
Service Employees International Union	60,498
Nurses Association of Ontario	52,055
Total Female Union Membership	1,511,113

* Estimated on the basis that the male/female ratio among provincial employees is approximately the same as among government unions generally.
** Figure in brackets includes five Ontario, Alberta, British Columbia and Quebec locals only. A national figure is not reported.
Source: Statistics Canada, *CALURA*, Pt. 2, 1989 (71-202)

cent female membership). These unions have been able to endure and grow despite the strong opposition of employers in the trade, clerical and service sectors to unionization. This was exemplified by the sustained anti-union campaigns by the banks and a major national department store chain in the 1980s.

We have only made the barest sketch of the trials and tribulations of union organization in those industrial and occupational areas where women workers have traditionally been concentrated. Like the history of the labour movement in Canada generally, it has been an uncertain and uneven record marked by both worker solidarity and factionalism across both political and sexual lines. Neither women nor immigrants were particularly well served, at least in the earlier periods, by organized labour. But this has changed quite remarkably in the last decade or so; and despite the obstacles, the history of employer resistance and the rise of neo-conservatism, the progress of unionism among women has been creditable in the last few decades — though much remains to be done.

Women and Unions: Today

Canada is not a highly unionized country, though there is considerable variation among regions. Table 6-3 gives some indication not only of the regional variation, but also of the variation between male and female workers. While women are significantly less organized than men, the gap has been narrowing fairly rapidly since the sixties, indicating that women are organizing at a faster pace than men in the last three decades. Between 1985 and 1989, the number of female paid workers rose by 15.8 per cent, the number of female union members by 20.1 per cent. In 1965 women represented only 17 per cent of union members. A decade later their proportion had jumped to 26 per cent, and by 1989 to 39 per cent, not that much below their representation in the labour force (46 per cent of paid workers). One reason for this has been the growth of public administration unions, where women constitute over 48 per cent of all members. However, given the very high rate of existing unionization in the public sector (79 per cent for all workers and 76 per cent for women in 1989) and stagnation in employment growth in this sector, the potential for any continuation of this trend is much reduced.

Women are also well represented in national unions where they comprise 45.5 per cent of union membership. They appear to be

Table 6-3

Percentage of Paid Workers Organized
by Province and Sex, 1989

% Paid Workers* Organized

Province	Total	Female	Male
Atlantic			
Newfoundland	49.7	39.8	57.5
Nova Scotia	31.1	26.2	35.1
New Brunswick	34.4	28.3	39.5
Prince Edward Island	24.9	25.2	24.6
Quebec	39.9	35.8	42.3
Ontario	31.4	26.0	36.0
Prairies			
Manitoba	36.6	33.8	39.1
Saskatchewan	32.1	31.7	32.5
Alberta	26.4	26.6	26.2
British Columbia	37.1	31.5	41.7
Canada	34.1	29.4	38.0

* Persons receiving remuneration from employers for labour or services (does not include the self-employed, with or without paid employees, and unpaid family workers).
Source: Statistics Canada, *CALURA*, Pt. 2, 1989 (71-202); *The Labour Force*, December 1989 (71-001).

particularly well organized in independent unions in the education and health sectors. Over half of female union members in 1989 were employed in the education and health industries. They are least represented in the international unions (less than 25 per cent women members) which tend to be restricted to the traditional male blue-collar and craft workers (such as construction). The major exception to this is the rapidly growing United Food and Commercial Workers in the service and trade sectors.

The increase in female union membership in recent years has also been accompanied by an increase in female participation in union leadership though women are still greatly underrepresented in executive positions, particularly in the international unions. In 1985, the last year that the information was published, women made up 36.5 per cent of union membership but held only 19.3 per cent of executive board positions. (Statistics Canada stopped publishing the data in 1985 because it did not have sufficient confidence in their accuracy.) In the international unions the comparable figures were 21.1 per cent of membership and 1.7 per cent of board positions. Moreover, the percentage of executive board positions held by women in 1985 had remained virtually unchanged since the 1970s. In some areas, however, much more progress has been made, including in a number of high-profile positions such as the presidency and vice-presidency of the CLC, the presidency of a number of provincial labour federations and city labour councils, and the chief executive position in the largest union in Canada, the Canadian Union of Public Employees (CUPE). Linda Briskin, in a 1990 article, reported that in 1986 "women represented 50 per cent of the membership in the Public Service Alliance of Canada (PSAC) and held 40 per cent of all executive positions (although 70 per cent of those were in the position of secretary)." Perhaps more indicative of changed union attitudes were the actions of the Ontario Federation of Labour in 1983 in creating five positions on its executive board specifically for women; and of the Canadian Labour Congress in 1984 in adopting a similar constitutional amendment providing for a minimum of six female vice-presidents. Many other labour bodies have since made similar provisions.

Despite this progress, however, there remain many barriers to the assumption of women to leadership roles in the labour movement. Many union structures and practices remain hierarchical and male dominated. Women in executive positions are frequently relegated to the role of looking after "women's issues" or are marginalized in women's committees and caucuses. But perhaps the biggest barrier is the double (or triple) burden of paid work, work in the home and work for the union. It arises from the union activist's work patterns combined with women's traditional role in the home. Staff representatives face a great deal of travel, long evenings or weekends in bargaining sessions and long hours on the job. Faced with additional home responsibilities, which their partners are often not prepared to share, few women are prepared to make the sacrifice, especially in the majority of unions where there is a preponderance of male members whose perceived interests may be quite different from those of women members. Julie White discusses this at length in her study of postal workers. In 1987 when women comprised almost 43 per cent of the union's membership, they held only 33 per cent of local presidencies, 29 per cent of full-time paid presidencies, and a mere 17 per cent of full-time elected officials at regional and national levels. Most of the women who were involved with the union were those relatively free of family responsibilities. Peter Warrian, a union official, has described the problem. Union leaders, he wrote,

> rise through this [hierarchical union] structure, through large amounts of hard work, commitment to the organization and "being a team player." At a practical level, this means being available to the organization 24 hours a day, being locked up in hotel rooms for weeks on end, endless travel and separation from families. This inherently assumes, if these men are "available," then they are not available to their families. Women and children are by definition placed in a subordinate role, subject to the organizational and leadership needs of the union. They are arbitrarily subject to transfers, disruption of home and school life, see their men rarely, and usually in a spaced-out condition, etc. Women trade unionists see all this, and are offended by it. Most reject it.

Almost certainly this has begun to change. Unions have worked to modify their own attitudes and those of their members. Other than the affirmative action provisions in union constitutions, perhaps the best evidence lies in labour's bargaining program. Kumar and Acri's study, for instance, shows that in the union contracts they surveyed in Ontario almost half contained provisions outlawing sexual discrimination, almost two-thirds required the acquisition of seniority during maternity leave, 70 per cent provided for leave for personal reasons, almost a quarter for leave for family illness, a third for VDT protection and for part-time workers' rights, and so on. This is a far cry from the results of Julie White's survey of contract provisions on women's issues that we reported on in the first edition. Obviously women's issues have a much higher priority now than they did even a decade ago.

Nevertheless, progress in certain areas has been slow, particularly in the critical area of child care. Less than half of 1 per cent of contracts covering 7 per cent of employees had provisions for child care though this omission is probably due more to employer opposition than union apathy. Similarly, provisions covering sexual harassment are relatively rare, covering less than 15 per cent of employees though, to be fair, sexual harassment is also covered by human rights legislation. Inclusion in collective agreements only means that sexual harassment is subject to the grievance procedure and arbitration, a much faster, cheaper and less onerous route than recourse to human rights tribunals.

If women have such positive attitudes to unions, if unions benefit them so, and if unions have come to accept the primacy of women's issues, why has union organization among women workers lagged behind that among men? The answer again lies in the labour market allocation of the female worker. This becomes clear from an analysis of Table 6-4.

The problem is that women are already relatively well organized in certain job ghettos where the overall level of organization is also relatively high — the public service, education, health, even light manufacturing. However, the sectors and occupations where unionization has failed to penetrate to any extent are exactly those with a high percentage of female workers — finance, trade, services other than education and health, and clerical occupations generally in all industrial sectors. Note that for most of the industrial sectors, the percentage of women organized is not materially different than for men and in services and finance are marginally higher.

In Julie White's 1980 study *Women and Unions*, five of the six manufacturing subsectors where women were a third or more of the total labour force in the subsector, the percentage of women unionized was greater than that of men (the one exception was the catchall group, miscellaneous manufacturing). In eight of the subsectors where women were less than a third of the employees, women were 47 to 85 per cent organized. Only in the remaining seven subsectors were women less organized than men and less organized than the labour force generally. Further, almost all of these seven subsectors employed fewer than 20 per cent women, meaning that most would be office workers rather than production workers. This points to the fact that industry and occupation, not sex directly, explain the lower degree of labour organization among women. Excepting teaching and health employees, therefore, our conclusion is much the same as Kumar and Cowan's. "The findings suggest that since professionals, clerical, and sales and service workers are less likely to be unionized than other workers, trade unions face an uphill task in organizing the unorganized women."

Table 6-4
Distribution of Female Membership by Selected Industry, 1989

Industry	% of female paid workers	% Union Membership in Industry		% Female Union Members	% Unionized
		Total	Female		Total (F)#
Public admin.	6.5	16.3	17.0	41.3	79.1 (76.3)
Light manuf.*	4.1	4.7	4.6	38.9	41.3 (33.3)
Services**	47.1	34.3	57.6	66.4	34.6 (35.9)
Education	9.9	16.2	23.9	58.5	73.2 (70.9)
Health	17.3	14.2	29.1	81.1	50.3 (49.5)
Other serv.	19.9	4.0	4.6	45.7	4.0 (6.7)
Retail trade	15.2	4.8	5.7	46.9	2.3 (11.0)
Finance	6.6	0.5	0.6	72.6	3.8 (3.9)
Other	14.2	39.4	14.5	14.1	20.4 (30.0)
Total	100.0	100.0	100.0	41.3	34.1 (29.4)

Figures in brackets are the percentages of women organized.
* Light manufacturing includes food and beverages, tobacco, leather, and textiles, knitting and clothing.
** Education and health comprise 57.7 per cent of all women employed in the services industries but 92 per cent of all women union members in services.
Source: Statistics Canada, *CALURA*, Pt. 2, 1989 (71-202)

This, however, only raises the further question of why these sectors and occupations are less likely to be unionized. The answer lies both in the history of trade union organization and in the relative market power and ideological opposition of employers. The first unions were in the skilled crafts, which were, as we have pointed out, largely male preserves. As industrial capitalism evolved, general unions — such as the Knights of Labor — emerged and tried to organize all workers, including women, as did the more militant industrial unions like the American Labour Union, the One Big Union, and the Industrial Workers of the World. The fact is that the industrial unions with their unskilled and semiskilled workers were no match for the combined opposition of employers and government who were dedicated to smashing any class-based unionism but were willing to make some compromises with the skilled workers, and their unions, which had the market power to extract concessions. Where most women were employed, they had no such power.

In general, less than 10 per cent of the workers were able to organize stable unions in the period before the emergence of the industrial unions in the late thirties and their consolidation during and after the Second World War. The major unions that did exist were concentrated where women had sparse representation: in the construction, metal and railway-running trades, and among the miners in the more isolated mining communities.

The logjam was broken with the formation of the CIO and the political realities of the wartime economy which gave labour increased leverage. Nevertheless, acceptance of unionism even then never extended to most service, clerical or financial workers or to public employees, and as employment levelled off in the industrial sector after the postwar boom, union membership stagnated. The second break-through came in the mid-sixties with a change in attitude and in legislation affecting public employees.

No such attitudinal change has occurred in that bastion of anti-unionism, the financial sector, or even in the large-scale trade sector. In 1977, among bank employees, 77 per cent were women, over two-thirds of whom earned less than $10,000 a year. This can be compared to the men employed in the banks, two-thirds of whom earned more than $10,000. Furthermore, women were restricted to dead-end positions with little opportunity for promotion and had few, if any, fringe benefits. Despite a change in the ruling of the Canada Labour Relations Board in 1977 permitting the organization of banks, branch by branch (rather than demanding the impossible task of organizing all branches of a bank simultaneously), and despite the considerable resources committed at various times by a number of unions and the Canadian Labour Congress (CLC), so far success has been minimal. In part the organizing effort in the late seventies and early eighties was hindered by inter-union conflict over jurisdiction, between unions such as the United Food and Commercial Workers, the Office and Professional Workers, the Canadian Union of Bank Employees, the CLC umbrella organization, the Bank Workers' Organizing Committee, and the "militant feminist" B.C. independent union, the Service, Office and Retail Workers Union of Canada.

However, it was the intransigent opposition of the banks that ultimately brought organizing to a virtual standstill. This is the case despite the fact that a number of banks were found guilty of a variety of unfair labour practices ranging from closing organized branches, discriminating in wage increases against union members, transferring individuals among branches to eliminate union majorities, to even the firing of union activists. At the time of the organizing drive, one-third of all unfair labour practice complaints before the Canadian Labour Relations Board involved the banks. They had initiated what Rosemary Warskett has called an "orgy of litigation," using the juridification of Canadian industrial relations to tie up the fledgling union locals in the courts. The local unions were also hindered by the fact that the average branch bank employed only 14 employees. With turnover rates of over 30 per cent per year, time delays were on the side of the employer. As a result, ten years after the first spurt of 174 bank unit certifications, only 62 (covering less than 1 per cent of bank branches) remained in effect, the most important being the CIBC Toronto Visa Centre with 400 employees.

For similar reasons, the success of organizing drives among the insurance and trust companies and the large retailers, excepting the major grocery chains, has been equally limited. This is perhaps best illustrated by the experience of two unions which attempted to organize Eaton's stores in Ontario and Manitoba in 1984-85. In March of 1984, a local of the Retail, Wholesale and Department Store Union (RWDSU) was certified at the Eaton's store in Brampton, Ontario. Within months it was followed by five other stores in St. Catherines, London, and three in Toronto, in total representing less than 10 per cent of Eaton's employees. The union began negotiations for a first contract but the company remained intransigent. On November 30th 1984, 1,500 employees at all six outlets went out on strike in support of higher wages, a decent pension and benefit plan, job security and a seniority system. The majority — an estimated 80 per cent — were women, two-thirds of them part-time workers. Average wages before the strike were reported at $5.50 to $6.00 per hour, pensions as low as $115 per month after 26 years service.

The company did not put a contract offer to the union until after 28 bargaining sessions and then, when it did, offered the union less than the employees had before the union was organized. Union claims that this amounted to refusal to bargain in good faith were dismissed by the Labour Relations Board which argued that the exercise of unequal bargaining power did not constitute an unfair labour practice — in effect, that might makes right! Nevertheless, the refusal of the company to budge turned the strike into a strike of recognition and, as one women put it, a strike about "freedom for women." The labour movement across the country rallied in support of the strikers and a boycott of Eaton's was organized which was eventually endorsed by the United and Roman Catholic Churches. After five-and-a-half months on the picket line, unable to shut the stores down due to strikebreakers, and facing the six-month deadline after which, under Ontario law, the strikers lost their legal right to be reinstated in their jobs, the union capitulated and accepted a contract that merely codified the pre-strike conditions. The international office of the union, recognizing that the capitulation would not be ratified by the strikers, but not wanting to lose the membership to the union rolls, signed the contract without putting it to a vote of the membership. Ten months after the contract went into effect, as soon as it was legal to do so, a group of dissenting and replacement workers applied for decertification. The vote, taken in February of 1987 went two to one (647 to 301) against the RWDSU and the union was decertified except at four small non-retail units.

In Brandon the situation was somewhat different because the NDP government in Manitoba had enacted first-contract legislation which provided for the imposition of a first contract by the Labour Board in order to prevent exactly the kind of "recognition strike" as occurred in Ontario. In this case, the union was the Manitoba (United) Food and Commercial Workers which was certified as bargaining agent for the almost 100 employees (over 80 per cent of them women and just over half of them part-time employees), at the Brandon store in October of 1984 after the union signed up three quarters of all of those eligible. A small minority of the employees who opposed the union took legal action which delayed negotiations but, in any case, the company showed little inclination to bargain seriously which again led to the union filing unfair labour charges before the Manitoba Labour Board. The pending hearing on the charge brought the company to the bargaining table on May 9, 1985 where the union was offered the "Ontario contract." It responded by asking the Labour Board to impose a first contract and on July 23rd the Board issued its decision providing for significant wage increases plus other benefits. When Eaton's appeal was rejected, the company announced that it would reduce its Brandon operation and lay off 49 employees, about half of the staff, most of them part-time.

The union did enter into further negotiations to prevent the lay-off but nothing was resolved before the dissident employees applied for decertification nine-months into the one-year contract. The vote in Brandon was somewhat closer than in Ontario with around 40 per cent backing the union. But the company's scare tactics worked and the union was decertified. In both Ontario and Manitoba, the battle for union recognition had once more been lost.

In the eighties, the environment for further organization turned even more unfriendly to labour than it had been in the preceding period. Economic recession and high unemployment in the early years of the decade was followed by "jobless growth," the accession to power of neo-conservatism and the "decade of greed," global restructuring and free trade agreements. This culminated in a major dismembering of Canada's manufacturing sector and a second debilitating economic downturn in the early nineties, again driving unemployment into double digits. The unfavourable economic climate was in most jurisdictions accompanied by retrenchment in the public sector and by what Panitch and Swartz have called the assault on trade union freedoms by government. What is perhaps most surprising is not why unionization has declined a few percentage points in recent years, but how well it has been maintained. This is particularly evident when one compares the Canadian labour movement with the American where the level of unionization has declined to only a half or less of the Canadian level.

The real barrier to unionization for women lies in the opposition of employers, given the vulnerable economic position of the employees, who face a large reserve army of unemployed ready to take their places in any confrontation. The use of replacement workers (strikebreakers or "scabs") often under the protection of the police, contracting-out, plant relocation in the anti-union southern United States or Mexico, threats of plant or store closure, the increased use of part-time labour and non-English (or non-French) speaking immigrant women, dispersal of work into employees' homes — all these and many more techniques have been used to obstruct organization, and break strikes and unions.

The bargaining power of women workers is frequently even more vulnerable to labour market conditions than is men's. The advent of microelectronic technology may only serve to reduce whatever bargaining power these workers have, particularly if significant amounts of word and data processing is relocated to employees' homes. In the highly fragmented and competitive service (including hospitality and tourism) and trade sectors, the potential appears even more bleak. Union organizing, even at the best of times, is a difficult and expensive business, and the prospect of organizing a large, and growing, number of small employers with a high turnover of staff and a high proportion of part-time workers is formidable. Nor is it clear that unionization could secure benefits for members commensurate with the effort, given the competitive conditions in so many of the unorganized sectors, the decline in employment standards and increased competition from low-wage countries and areas. The ultimate loser in this economic milieu is the employee, a disproportionate number of whom are women. While it is important to amend our legislation to remove the barriers to organization of all workers, it may be that the only action that can give any security and support to these workers is upward revision of the minimum wage and improved labour standards legislation.

The future of women and unions? The evidence suggests that women benefit from organizing and that the benefit is, in most cases, substantial. Whether this will continue to be true if and when unionization spreads to those competitive and small-scale job markets where so many are employed is another question. But the recent evidence at least suggests that male unionists — or at least their leadership — have recognized their vested interest in promoting equal wages and working conditions for their female co-workers, if only to protect themselves from being undercut. The reasons are that the direction of structural and technological change and the resulting decline in jobs in primary and secondary goods production, combined with equal opportunity legislation and the penetration of more women into non-traditional jobs, threaten to increase competition between men and women for jobs, competition that employers can exploit in a sexually divided labour force. Human rights legislation and the Charter of Rights, in any case, make it considerably more difficult for men to resort to exclusionist tactics to counteract that competition. Given the further evidence that families increasingly need a second income to maintain their living standards, this means that men have a powerful additional motive to improve the economic status of women whether through inclusion in the unions or through active support for social and labour legislation that incorporates the women's agenda.

7

The Future: Proposals and Prospects for Change

The Challenge

Women's place in the world of work, despite the not inconsequential advances that women have made over the last two decades, remains that of a secondary citizen. One should not, however, downplay the progress that has been made. Over the decade of the eighties average female incomes increased from less than half those of men to almost 60 per cent, average earnings from 51.6 to 59.9 per cent, and the earnings of full-time, full-year women workers, from 64.2 to 67.6 per cent of male earnings. Moreover, legislation has been passed in several jurisdictions promoting pay and employment equity, thereby extending human rights legislation and the Charter of Rights; and it is clear that unions, for the most part, have accepted gender equality as a priority in collective bargaining and in legislative lobbying. The numbers and percentages of female engineers, scientists and professionals are rising, albeit slowly and from an almost inconsequential base. Perhaps the most encouraging sign has been the steady increase of women in managerial and administrative occupations, from 16 to 45 per cent over the past two decades, even if many of these are subordinate positions. Also, family laws have been amended to provide for equal splitting of family assets on marriage breakdown. While these improvements can hardly satisfy those interested in the rapid achievement of gender equality, they do represent substantial progress.

There is no reason, however, to be sanguine or complacent. There are new and disturbing developments, one of the most serious being the "feminization of poverty". As we state in Chapter 3, it results from the continuing high levels of marriage breakdown and single parentage, the lack of adequate support payments and day care for working mothers, and the increasing reliance on part-time work. A

second development is the rise in inequality and the polarization of
the entire labour market that is resulting from the destruction of
middle-income jobs in the goods-producing industries combined
with the creation of a large number of low-level, service jobs and a
considerably smaller number of technical, skilled and professional
jobs. The prevalence of these phenomena was documented in a 1988
Statistics Canada study by Myles, Picot and Wannell which covered
the period from 1981 to 1986:

> Our main conclusion is that the distribution of wages (across
> all age groups) did become somewhat more polarized over
> this period. … [T]he main change, which occurred across the
> entire economy, was a decline in the relative wage rates in
> jobs held by young people, on one hand, and on the other, if
> anything an increase in the relative wage rates in jobs held by
> middle-aged workers.

From a woman's perspective this is not encouraging since it means
that *new* job creation (entry positions) is at the very bottom wage
category, which will adversely affect the higher proportion of first-
time female labour market entrants. It should also be noted that
almost 60 per cent of jobs occupied by young women (under 25
years) were in the lowest wage categories compared with a much
smaller 44 per cent for young men. At the other end of the age and
wage scale, the results were not much more encouraging. High-
wage jobs declined by almost a third for both men and women in the
25 to 34 age group and while wages paid to both men and women in
the 35 to 49 age group rose substantially, the proportional increase
in the numbers of women affected was only around half that of men.
Furthermore, for those 50 years of age and older, only men benefited from upward wage mobility.

The polarization of the labour market is in part the result of the
growth in employment in the low-paid service sectors and the decline
in employment in the higher paying goods-producing sectors. But as
Myles, Picot and Wannell point out, this is not the major cause of
the growing polarization. The major cause is that entry jobs *in all
industries* are paying lower wages; and the dismembering of job
ladders in the lower tier of the primary labour market means that
upward mobility is becoming increasingly difficult for those not
already on the ladder. For most women workers and all younger
workers, this is not good news. It is also bad news for workers being

laid off due to "restructuring" and the decline of traditional manufacturing and for women who are attempting to re-enter the labour market after a period of non-participation due to family responsibilities.

The reasons for this decline in new "good jobs" is associated with the processes we described in Chapters 5 and 6, increased competition from low-wage countries and regions, free trade, market deregulation, privatization, public sector retrenchment, and the assault on union organization — all elements of the neo-conservative policy agenda. The decline has also been intensified by recent deep recessions beginning in 1981 and 1990, whose recoveries were delayed and attenuated by this same neo-conservative program and by the accompanying fiscal and monetary policies.

At the same time, if female participation rates continue to rise at a rate similar to that of the last three decades — particularly in the face of stagnation, even decline, in public sector employment, and a slower rate of growth, stagnation or decline in clerical occupations with the spread of microelectronic technology — there will likely be both a significant increase in female unemployment and considerable downward pressure on female wage rates on the presumption of a continuing gender-based job distribution.

This rather pessimistic forecast is based on the premise that social attitudes towards the role of women (what political conservatives call "family values"), held not only by men but by many women as well, have not changed sufficiently to accommodate the kind of pro-active programs required if progress toward gender equality is not to become stalled. In this view, it is considered unlikely that attitudes will change much in the near future, especially in an economic climate of depressed economic opportunity. It is much easier to promote a change in distribution of economic opportunity and income in a climate of economic growth than in one of stagnation or decline.

Is this assessment excessively pessimistic? The signs at the moment are obviously mixed. On the negative side are phenomena such as the continuing high level of violence against women and of sexual harassment in the workplace, cutbacks in social, health and educational programs (particularly the retraction of the Mulroney government's promise of a national day-care program), the feminization of poverty, the double disadvantage of the growing number of immigrant women and women of visible minorities, the political power of religious fundamentalism and anti-abortion organizations, the stagnation and underrepresentation in the number of women on corporate boards, in Parliament, legislatures and other political bodies, the attacks on unionism and collective bargaining, and business opposition to the extension of pay and employment equity to the private sector. Perhaps most ominous is the expected consequence of the Canada-United States Free Trade Agreement and North America Free Trade Agreement in forcing the harmonization of Canadian with American and Mexican social policy, which would undermine even existing programs.

More positively, however, we must note the strength and vitality of the women's movement in Canada and the emergence within a resilient labour movement of women in leadership positions and of women's issues in the labour agenda. Furthermore, the legislative achievements of the last decade or so — in the Charter of Rights, in human rights legislation at both the provincial and federal levels, in affirmative action and in pay equity — will not be easily reversed. There is also some indication that the North American public's disaffection with the economic woes initiated by the neo-conservative economic agenda may have reversed the swing of the political pendulum so that it is now moving in a more socially conscious direction.

It is in this climate that the movement to advance the cause of female equality must operate. Our purpose here is to look at and evaluate a number of the proposals that have been put forward to improve women's position in the Canadian political economy. In the final analysis, equality will only be achieved when fundamental institutions and attitudes in our society are altered. Discrimination against women is ingrained in our social and economic systems, so deeply imbedded that equality will not be easily achieved by any number of specific remedial provisions, no matter how well intentioned. Basic to a systemic change must be the acceptance by men that the work in the home is not "woman's work" but work to be shared. Until the added burden of household work is removed from being the sole responsibility of women, there can be little hope for true equality in the marketplace.

Proposals for Change

There is little reason to believe that the gains won by women over the past two decades will necessarily be consolidated and continued

without further action. Social change, particularly of such a fundamental nature as is involved in raising women to equality, does not
take place simply with a recognition of the problem. It will only
take place under strong pressure. This makes it mandatory that, if
further progress is to be achieved, an aggressive and progressive
women's movement be maintained. This also requires that its base
of support be continually broadened and renewed by coalition
building with other sympathetic popular organizations, particularly
those with a base in the working-class which has borne the brunt of
the costs of restructuring.

Obviously, the struggles for women's reproductive rights and
control over their bodies, equality in appointments to political,
cultural and judicial office, freedom from violence and sexual harassment and recognition of political and social equality are important
and must continue. But important as these goals may be, they also
require a material or economic base. By this we mean that without
access to equal opportunities and economic returns in the labour
market, women will have difficulty escaping the dependency that
underpins many of the other aspects of gender subordination and
inequality. This, in turn, requires a number of immediate economic
reforms to deal with the sources of inequality in the labour market
that we have identified here.

Over the longer run, creating a climate for permanent change will
depend on a moderation in people's attitudes, a long and slow
process of education, not only in the formal system (changing
textbook stereotypes, bringing equality into school counselling,
incorporating in syllabi female role models, and so on), but also
across the broad spectrum of information media, including TV with
its pervasive influence in shaping social attitudes and creating
stereotypes. Nevertheless, even with evolving attitudes, change will
be manifested in a number of discrete measures, many of them
legislative. A number of such measures have been proposed: wages
for house workers; equal pay for work of equal value (pay equity);
affirmative action (employment equity); a major expansion of public
day care; pension reforms; the encouragement of unionization in the
service industries; and a significant upward revision in labour standards, in particular the minimum wage, and the expansion of all labour
standards coverage to part-time workers. We will examine these
proposals.

House Workers' Wages

One of the earliest proposals of some women's groups, rarely heard these days, was for the payment of wages to any person, male or female, acting as a full-time homemaker, much as family allowance used to be paid. Though there is no reason that this should apply only to women, in our contemporary society the vast majority of people who would be affected are women. This proposal has many attractive features. It would give women, particularly those in poorer families and those with preschool-age children, a real choice between work in the home and work in the labour market. In turn, this would reduce the reserve supply of women to the labour market and lighten downward pressure on women's wages. Housewives would have an income independent of money provided by their husbands, which would not only reduce their dependency, but also increase their sense of self-worth. This would also have the benefit of reducing women's vulnerability to spousal abuse and desertion. The drawbacks, however, are that the proposal would also likely perpetuate the sexual division of labour in the household with its consequences for sexual stereotyping of jobs in the labour market, and would encourage women to withdraw from the labour market for family rearing with the resultant negative consequences for career and income progression.

Whatever its merits, however, the proposal is not likely to receive serious consideration. It would involve new government transfer spending of at least $30 billion (1992) a year without any *real* increase in economic output. The only way to finance such a payment would be a massive increase in taxes on those in the labour market. This would be at a time when the state is already facing a self-pro-claimed fiscal crisis and tax revolts from increasingly burdened consumers are becoming common. At the same time the corporate sector has steadily decreased its proportional contribution to tax revenues, a transfer of the tax burden likely to be accelerated by free trade. Furthermore, the Mulroney government has just finished curtailing family allowances, the one social program that most closely approached that of a houseworker's wage, and opposes the very principle of such universal programs. Given the political climate, therefore, wages for housework would appear to be a "non-starter," at least for the foreseeable future.

Pay and Employment Equity

Equal pay for equal work has been a traditional demand of unions since the last century, but it was not until 1956 that it was achieved at the federal level in Canada, when the Canadian government, over the opposition of private employers, passed equal pay legislation covering the 10 per cent of the labour force under its jurisdiction. As we have noted, the major purpose of the unions in advocating equal pay was to protect male workers from competition from lower-wage female workers. In short, it was primarily an exclusion device, though when implemented it did protect women from the most blatant forms of wage discrimination and for this reason always commanded the support of women's organization. During the 1960s and '70s, legislation providing for equal pay for "equal work," "equivalent work," "similar or substantially similar work" (the different wordings used in different jurisdictions) became general across the country.

However, despite some notable breakthroughs (such as the determination that the work of nurses' aids is equal to that of orderlies, or that the work of librarians is equal to that of archivists, to cite two high-profile court decisions), the impact of equal pay legislation had minimal effects in decreasing male-female wage and earnings differentials. This is because any differences in skill, responsibility, effort, or working conditions, whether inherent in the jobs or deliberately designed into jobs to make them appear significantly different, were frequently held to render the work unequal and not subject to the equal pay provisions. Secondly, the provisions only hold for the same employer in the same plant and location, a weakness of all attempts to legislate wage equality.

To address the first problem, women's organizations, increasingly supported by the unions, have called for equal pay for work of equal value. In Canada the concept of equal pay for work of equal value is now usually referred to as *pay equity*, which (as Judy Fudge and Patricia McDermott point out in *Just Wages*, their assessment of the contemporary state of pay equity), emphasizes the *goal* of wage equality as compared with the U.S. usage of "comparable worth" which emphasizes the *process* of achieving wage parity. The concept of pay equity is now embodied in legislation in eight jurisdictions in Canada, six provinces, the Yukon Territory, and the federal government through the Human Rights Act. However, the federal, Yukon and Quebec legislation is complaint-based, which means that individual employees or groups of employees must file a complaint with the human rights agency against a particular employer alleging discrimination. This contrasts with the pro-active Pay Equity Acts, first initiated by the NDP government of Manitoba in 1985 and which by 1989 had spread to Ontario, Nova Scotia, Prince Edward Island, and New Brunswick, which requires specified employers to initiate action to bring about pay equity. Moreover, Ontario made world history when it extended pay equity to the private sector and not just to public employees within its jurisdiction. In addition, British Columbia and Newfoundland have adopted non-statute, pay equity policies within their civil services.

There are many limitations to current pay equity programs, apart from the fact that only five are pro-active and only one includes the private sector. The first we have already mentioned, the fact that pay equity is generally restricted to individual, large employers and single locations. Secondly, the definition of fe-male- or male-dominated job classes is determined by threshold values (usually 60 or 70 per cent female or male), which may exclude some affected groups, while comparison requires the existence of an appropriate male-dominated job class. Thirdly, the basis for determining equity is usually job evaluation using four basic criteria — skill, effort, responsibility, working conditions — which critics charge are themselves not gender-neutral. The values placed on them, they argue, are values created by male-dominated markets and therefore tend to overvalue criteria char-acteristic of male work. Also, they reinforce male-dominated hierarchical management. Nevertheless, the very concept of pay equity does challenge the market as the sole determinant of women's wages, at the same time as it legitimizes the market determination of male job values.

Perhaps the most serious limitation of pay equity, however, is that even if it were universal and effective, it would leave untouched most of the earnings differential between men and women. As we noted earlier, wage discrimination is estimated to account for only four or five percentage points of the overall difference of around 40 per cent. This is confirmed by the extent of earnings narrowing when pay equity programs have been introduced in some jurisdictions al-though in others, the narrowing has been somewhat higher (around 10 per cent in the Prince Edward Island civil service). This, of course, is no reason not to press for universal, pro-active pay equity. But it does emphasize the importance of other measures to reduce the discrepancy between male and female earnings, particularly employment equity.

Employment equity involves creating equal opportunity for all people for employment in all occupations and at all levels. Specifically, it prohibits discrimination in hiring and employment practices (systemic discrimination) and, in its pro-active form (affirmative action), provides for deliberate over-hiring of underrepresented groups. While all provinces prohibit discrimination on the basis of race, sex, religion or other individual characteristic through human rights legislation, and many have specific affirmative action programs dealing with particular target groups (normally women, aboriginals, visible minorities, and the disabled), and particular occupations (police, hydro construction, and teachers being some specific cases), only the federal government has so far addressed employment equity in a systematic way through employment equity legislation. Ontario is expected to soon follow suit.

Like the provinces, the original federal government legislation affecting employment equity was through human rights legislation. The 1977 Canadian Human Rights Act and Human Rights Commission prohibited discriminatory employment programs and provided for the Commission to investigate complaints and initiate remedies where warranted. The legislation and the Canadian Charter of Rights also provided that affirmative action programs (preferences) for disadvantaged target groups, including women, do not constitute discrimination.

In 1986, the federal government passed the Employment Equity Act. It goes much farther than the Human Rights Act in that it requires employers (including federal departments) to: i. report on their employment of women, visible minorities, aboriginals and the disabled; ii. identify and eliminate barriers to the employment of these groups; iii. prepare affirmative action plans detailing how and when representative workforces will be achieved; and iv. institute affirmative action policies to ensure that these groups are adequately represented in their workforces — though only in the case of reporting is enforcement provided for. These provisions cover all employers with 100 or more employees under federal jurisdiction. Though the Act does not require it, the Human Rights Commission also requests comparable information from the Treasury Board and the Public Service Commission for the federal civil service and government agencies. Similar requirements are also required of employers, otherwise under provincial jurisdiction, who are doing or seeking business with the federal government under the contractors program administered by Canada Employment and Immigration Commission. The Human Rights Commission, which oversees the reporting requirements of the Act, has operated primarily through joint reviews with employers of their employment situation rather than through complaints and litigation. As of January 1992, twenty-five joint reviews affecting roughly two-thirds to three-quarters of the workforce covered had been undertaken, fourteen with firms under the Employment Equity Act, eleven with federal departments and agencies. Where the situation is deemed not to measure up to the goals established in the legislation (essentially that the workforce have the same relative composition of the designated group as is in the labour force available to it) a plan is negotiated designed to achieve employment equity. The plan may include special recruitment, training and promotion programs, the changing of stated job or physical qualifications, and education and sensitizing initiatives to make employers and managers more aware of the problems encountered by the target groups and more supportive of their needs. The Commission then monitors the implementation of the plan for a period of three years.

The provisions of the federal and provincial acts suffer the same weaknesses of any complaint based system in that they are reactive rather than pro-active and are difficult to enforce. In the first instance, very few employees are willing to take the risk of making a complaint. It is time consuming and uncertain. The burden of proof is frequently on the employee, and discrimination is difficult, often nearly impossible, to prove. Also, it often depends on women applying for positions or promotions in non-traditional areas. Consequently, there have been a very low number of complaints brought to provincial or federal boards. The federal commission, for instance, had 73 complaints by 1992 under the Employment Equity Act of which only 11 came from individuals. All but two of the rest came from two organizations, the Assembly of Manitoba Chiefs and the Disabled People for Employment Equity Human Rights Group. The remaining two were initiated by the Human Rights Commission itself.

Despite the weaknesses of the complaint system and employer hostility to the program, including eight court challenges to the authority of the Commission, it has been judged by the Conference Board of Canada to have had a significant effect on employment practices in federally regulated businesses, particularly for women, and to have raised the profile of employment equity among business leaders. Indeed, 84 per cent of the federally regulated organizations surveyed indicated that they had initiated some form of employment equity program by the end of 1990. Nevertheless, there are other indications that the program is failing to achieve the equal opportunity goal. In 1990, women who represented 44 per cent of the available labour force according to the 1986 Census, represented 43.7 per cent of employees covered by the Employment Equity Act and 44.4 per cent of employees of federal departments. However, women were still largely concentrated in clerical and administrative support categories. They were poorly represented in transportation and mining and in non-traditional manual work. They remain grossly underrepresented among directors, executives and senior managers. In 1990, according to a recent study by Professor Lauzon, women accounted for only 4.7 per cent of directorships of major public and Crown corporations and only 6.7 per cent of top executive positions. The financial sector has been one of the worst offenders along with the resource and industrial products industries. In federal departments and agencies, the situation is only marginally better where the Human Rights Commission reported that women held only 15 per cent of the management jobs in 1990.

Although union leadership has indicated support for mandatory affirmative action, it does run up against worker hostility to any scheme that would abrogate the hard-fought-for seniority system. Indeed, a backlash among employees has been reported by a large number of employers implementing such action. However, this may in part be attributed to the fact that unions and employee organizations have been largely excluded from the design and implementation of these programs even though their inclusion is mandated by the Employment Equity Act. Without employee participation, opposition to any management-imposed plan can be expected. When the regulations are promulgated for the Ontario employment equity program, we may expect more significant labour involvement.

Still, it is readily apparent that without affirmative action, progress in opening up equal opportunity will be both slow and partial; and inequity in employment opportunities is deemed responsible for approximately a quarter to a third of male-female earnings differentials, or two to three times the effect of wage discrimination. The obvious place to begin is at the provincial level with governments and Crown corporations. But despite all the criticisms made of government, there is evidence that it is already a more equalitarian employer than the private sector, at least with respect to gender. Employment equity, therefore, needs to be extended to the private sector. Federal, provincial and municipal governments can utilize the weapon of contract compliance to enforce affirmative action in much of the private sector. This has been introduced at both federal and provincial levels in Canada with respect to native workers in a number of northern energy projects, and more generally, in Quebec and in Toronto. It could be generalized to include female workers in all contracts at all levels of government.

The problem is primarily one of political will and of enforcement, particularly in non-traditional occupations where a skilled female labour force does not now exist. This would require a substantial expansion of programs to train women in these non-traditional jobs. Unfortunately, this comes at a time when the federal government is drastically cutting its expenditures in employment training and shuffling its responsibilities in this area off to the provinces. It will also require a significant improvement in the state of the Canadian economy (as of the early nineties). There is little prospect that employers or unions will accept, or indeed even be in a position to offer, affirmative action employment policies in a period of very high unemployment, layoffs and shutdowns. Women, therefore, have a vested interest in reversing the neo-conservative economic agenda that has contributed substantially to the high unemployment rates that make unfeasible and politically unacceptable the expansion of affirmative action.

Pension Reform

There are two reasons to support the call for reforms in the pension system. The first is simply one of correcting the injustice suffered by many women as a result of biases in the way the current system works. The second is that it is a necessary precondition to reducing the extent of female poverty. The fundamental problem is that, with the exception of the Old Age Pensions (OAS), Guaranteed Income Supplement (GIS) and related Spouse's Allowance, most pension income is earnings- and employment-related. As a result, women face two disadvantages. The most obvious is the inferior lifetime earnings capacity of most women workers as a consequence of both lower wages and incomes and also of interrupted careers and a shorter working life. If women choose not to enter the paid labour force but opt instead to work full-time in the home, they earn no pension entitlement at all in their own right but must rely on spousal benefits where available.

The second disadvantage is that private, occupation-based pension plans, which are assumed to account for three-quarters of earnings-based pension income, covered less than 40 per cent of women workers in 1987, (the latest published data), compared with over half of men. Also, part-time workers, the majority of whom are women, are very poorly served by private pension plans. Only 16 per cent of part-time women workers had pension coverage in 1987. Thus women are less likely to be entitled to any earnings-related pension income; but even when they are, the pensions are generally much lower than men's. In theory, of course, it is possible for workers, male or female, to provide for their own pensions through Registered Retirement Savings Plans (RRSPs). However, this is not an option that is in reality applicable to lower income workers, women house workers, or part-time workers. It is mainly a tax-financed benefit for the upper income bracket and for self-employed businessmen and professionals.

The inadequacies in the present pension system have been addressed in a 1990 report of the National Council of Welfare, *Pension Reform*. Many of the recommendations included in the report are directly relevant to disadvantages faced by women. They are grouped into three categories: improving the basic non-earnings related income security programs (including a return to universality in the Old Age Pension and abolition of the clawbacks); improving and extending the Canada and Quebec Pension Plans; and reforming the private-sector pension plans (including RRSPs).

Although the provision of the GIS has considerably reduced the problem of seniors' poverty, the level is still insufficient to raise the poor senior who does not have an outside income or other pension above the poverty line. In 1989, Old Age Security and GIS together provided only 72 per cent of the poverty line for a single person in a large city. Since women are far more likely than men to be in this situation and to be without alternative outside income, the proposed rise in the GIS for this poorest of groups is an obvious first step. The problem of poverty for married couples is not quite as severe, although if a couple must rely wholly on OAS, the GIS and Spouse's Allowance, their annual income would still have fallen almost two thousand dollars below the poverty line in 1989. Therefore, there is need for an increase in the GIS and Spouse's Allowance for this group as well, though not perhaps as large. The National Council on Welfare also proposes extension of Spouse's Allowances to all poor Canadians over the age of sixty to end the age discrimination in the existing plan. For instance, women sixty to sixty-four who are divorced or separated remain ineligible for spouse's allowance. Finally, the Council argues that the clawbacks on old age pensions be repealed and universality be restored. Instead, the tax system should be reformed to tax *all* sources of retirement income equally. This, of course would apply to all incomes, male, female and family.

The universal public employment-related pension plans, the Canada Pension Plan (CPP) and its Quebec equivalent, the Quebec Pension Plan (QPP) also need to be reformed. As previously noted, when these plans were established in 1966 they were designed to provide only one-quarter of the expected income necessary for a decent retirement standard of living. The other 75 per cent was expected to come from private pension plans and other savings and investments. However, as we have also noted, less than half the labour force, only 38.7 per cent of women, and only 16 per cent of women part-time employees (1987) have private pension plan coverage, while RRSPs and other private investment income is primarily restricted to upper income earners, businessmen and independent professionals. Women especially, therefore, are not well served by the existing pension system. But, to be fair, neither are men. A single person receiving the *maximum* CPP or QPP pension as well as Old Age Security and Guaranteed Income Supplement would have had an income that in 1989 barely exceeded the poverty level. A couple in the same situation would have been only marginally better off. Anybody with less than the average wage, and this would disproportionately include women because of their lower wages and lifetime earnings, would be in an even worse position and could fall below the poverty line despite thousands of dollars of income supplement payments.

The National Council of Welfare's recommendation to remedy this situation is to sharply increase the value of pensions under the CPP and QPP plans, to 50 per cent of retirement income for lower income people. This would not only give many more pensioners incomes significantly above the poverty line but would also substantially reduce government transfers in the form of GIS payments. Women, including those with an occupational history of part-time and low-wage work, would be clear beneficiaries.

Other recommendations of the Council for changes to the CPP

designed to improve the status of women include making the splitting of pension credits automatic and mandatory in the case of
marriage breakdown. As it is now, although the plan does require
that pension credits be split equally on family dissolution, the
Canada Pension Plan also requires that applications for credit-splitting be filed. By 1989 such applications had been filed in less than
5 per cent of divorce cases according to the Council's report.

The report also recommends credit-splitting be required in all
provincial and federal jurisdictions for private, occupational pension
plans. But what is perhaps most urgent is the need to require all such
plans to include continuing benefits for surviving spouses — which
in the majority of cases will be women. As it is now, most private
pension plans make no provision for survivor benefits.

Unless such reforms are made, the spectre of poverty among older
women will remain ever present. However, what is also required is
the expansion of occupational plans to a much higher percentage of
the labour force, in particular to part-time workers. The best way to
achieve this is through the encouragement of unions and collective
bargaining, since fringe benefits, including pension plans, are much
more prevalent in unionized firms than they are in non-union firms.
For instance, in 1978 the average unionized firm spent almost three
times as much on pensions and welfare plans as did non-unionized
firms (reported in Morley Gunderson and Craig Riddell's *Labour
Market Economics*). In addition to raising women's wages and
reducing wage discrimination, therefore, unions have the additional
benefit of improving women's economic position in old age.

Day Care and Parental Leave

Of all the legislative measures important to the future economic
status of women, the expansion of subsidized day-care facilities
(along with relevant parental leave provisions) is perhaps the most
important. The evidence given in Chapter 3 strongly supports the
argument that it is the interruption of women's careers that constitutes a major barrier to female equality in the marketplace. Career
interruption forces women to start all over again on re-entry to the
market even when they are able to climb onto a job ladder. It denies
women seniority and the on-the-job training so central to productivity. It encourages statistical discrimination by employers. And it
contributes to the poverty problem among low-income and female-

headed, single-parent families. Maternity leave, now widely available, does provide some protection for women for a relatively brief time surrounding the birth date, but does little for the more prolonged period of infant and child rearing. Also, the cost of private day care in simple monetary terms or the lack of care and supervision that so often accompanies the alternative informal child-care arrangements, acts as a formidable barrier to women in lower-paying jobs.

This is not only our conclusion. "Child care," Gunderson, Muszynski and Keck conclude, "is an essential support for women and all parents who work in the labour market.... A strategy is required to expand the number of licensed child-care spaces dramatically...." What they propose includes a major capital grants program for constructing child-care facilities and the creation of a refundable tax credit for child-care. The fact, however, is that the Mulroney Conservative government has reneged on its promise to establish a national child-care program. On the other hand, from women's point of view, it is fortunate that the provisions of the 1992 constitutional accord, which would have made it much more difficult to introduce such a new national social program, were defeated.

Good quality, low-cost day care is, of course, no panacea. It is of little use to women who choose to be full-time housewives during the child-rearing period. It is also not without its detractors, particularly those who argue that young children need a mother in the home in their formative years to develop personally and socially. But even if this were the case, and it is by no means generally accepted, the facts are that many women, for reasons of need or of choice, must and will work, if not full-time, at least part-time. It makes a great deal more sense to provide quality day care at a cost that ensures a reasonable take-home income than to continue with grossly inadequate day care that leaves women workers with minimal incomes after care costs have been paid.

A further issue is whether day care should be community based — that is, located in the home community — or if it should be employment based — located at the place of employment of either the mother or father. Both have their advantages, but in the case of large employers there is much to be said for employment-based care, both for the parent in the form of proximity and convenience, and also for the employer: employers with such facilities report a significant decline in turnover and absenteeism; more women are able and willing to work full-time or on shifts; maternity leaves are shorter; and productivity in some cases has risen.

On the other hand, some concern has been expressed that employer-tied day care not only raises the problems of the children's proximity to industrial pollution and hierarchical authority structures, but may also result in subsidization of employers by employees through lower wages made possible by the reduced mobility of workers.

Thus, day-care issues are not unequivocally resolved. It would still be undeniable, however, that quality, low-cost day care is a necessary condition for lessening the economic burden of child rearing on women. Given the totally inadequate facilities at present, as indicated by the imbalance between the number of spaces and the number of preschool children of working women, one should expect that the provision of day care will remain foremost among people concerned with the women's movement.

We have not discussed many of the other, less central suggestions to facilitate improvement in the economic status of women: for example, parental leave on the European model, which provides for a number of days' leave a year from work for family duties for both men and women, placing men on the same footing as women before employers; or flexitime, which permits adaptation of working hours around family schedules, and work sharing, which permits people to share a full-time, regular job — both measures that would increase the ability of women to cope with dual jobs in and out of the home and allow men to share more equitably in work in the home. The list is not meant to be exhaustive. However, it does touch on the most important provisions that could be made and, if they are to benefit all women in the labour force, must be achieved through government action. For some women, of course, many of these reforms may be achieved through union action.

Unions

Unions have been criticized in the past for being male dominated and male oriented — exclusionist of women and uninterested in the so-called "women's issues" in collective bargaining, unconcerned with organizing women and unsupportive of women involved in industrial disputes. From our historical review it is apparent that unions have had a rather chequered history with respect to organizing, supporting and promoting women in the labour movement. Even now, we would not suggest that all unions, on all issues, are always totally supportive of women. However, it is equally apparent that the labour movement as a whole has made great progress within the last decade or so in accepting the principles of feminism and of women's equality in the labour market. Even the problems that remain, we would argue, do not represent failings peculiar to unions but rather reflect the same economic and social forces that produced the inferior economic position of women in the first place.

In fact, the evidence presented in Chapter 6 documents that unions do benefit women substantially in terms of wages, working conditions and fringe benefits and in reducing inequality in wages and promotions. Unions have been a major driving force in achieving recognition and acceptance of some fundamental women's demands, including maternity leave benefits, equal pay for work of equal value, and health and safety in the electronic office. Secondly, there is considerable evidence that unions and their officials are much more sympathetic to and cognizant of women's issues than are employers. This was brought out in a study done for Canada Employment and Immigration as early as 1979. Trade unionists were four times as likely to identify women as a leading disadvantage group than were the sample of contractors and manufacturers interviewed, and they were the least likely to consider women the least disadvantaged of all minority groups.

Of course, actions speak louder than words. As pointed out in Chapter 6, female wages are consistently higher and male/female wage differentials are in almost all cases lower among unionized workers than among those non-unionized. But the effect of unions goes beyond purely monetary issues. As Kumar and Acri have pointed out, "[S]exual and racial equality is [now] an integral part of the Canadian labour movement's economic and social policy agenda." For instance, unionized workers are much more likely to have provisions superior to those of non-unionized workers with respect to maternity leave, fringe benefits for part-time workers, child-care leave and allowances, protection from sexual harassment, day care, affirmative action, non-discriminatory promotion and promoting pay and employment equity. Many examples can be given, particularly in the public sector where women represent a higher proportion of the union membership. (A fuller list and examples can be found in Kumar and Acri's 1991 study, "Women's Issues and Collective Bargaining.")

Furthermore, women and feminist consciousness have made considerable gains within the leadership of the unions within the last fifteen years. As one labour and feminist activist, Linda Briskin, has noted "although the numbers of women leaders have not increased as quickly as we might like, feminist-informed leadership practices in the union movement are having an important impact, and have the potential to inspire a creative rethinking of union organization."

Moreover, the labour movement's impact goes beyond collective bargaining. Outside of the women's movement itself, unions have been the most active bodies in lobbying governments for progressive legislation that would advance women's economic and social interests, particularly in such areas as pensions, minimum wages and other labour standards, occupational health and safety, crisis centres, day care, restrictions on sub-contracting, and pay and employment equity. On broader policy issues affecting women, labour has been at the forefront of opposition to the free trade agreements, deregulation, privatization and the retrenchment of social services and universal programs.

What are the prospects for expanding unionism, particularly in sales, service and clerical occupations; the finance, insurance and real estate and trade industries; and among part-time workers — all employment areas where women are concentrated and where unionization rates are low? The fact is that under existing legislation it is difficult. The reasons are generally recognized: strong employer opposition, fragmentation and small size of employee groups, high turnover among women workers, high proportion of part-time workers, employment instability, highly competitive market climate, low skill content of jobs, high labour to capital ratios, attitudes toward unions among women workers, deference of women to male hierarchical management, and so on. It may very well be impossible to unionize in some sectors or with some employers, and therefore improvements may only be gained through upgraded labour standards. However, for others unionization would be possible and should be encouraged by legislative changes that would make organization less difficult and would make arriving at a collective agreement a less conflictual and, at times, violent process.

In their discussions of how to combat female poverty among the working poor, Gunderson, Muszynski and Keck recommend six specific governmental changes. These include: i. creating a positive climate toward unions; ii. restricting contracting out; iii. limiting the right of employers to threaten or carry out plant closures to escape unionization; iv. imposing first contracts where employers refuse to negotiate; v. prohibiting strikebreakers ("replacement workers" or "scabs"); and vi. introducing sanctions against employers who refuse to bargain meaningfully ("in good faith"). There are others we would add. It is obvious from the experience with the banks that procedures must be found to prevent employers from interfering with the employees' right to organize through threats, transfers, other forms of unfair labour practice, and refusal to provide lists of eligible employees. Perhaps this could best be accomplished by setting much higher penalties for unfair labour practices and allowing automatic certification where such practices occur. Secondly, we view favourably the Manitoba experience with final-offer-selection (FOS) arbitration to settle disputes in just those kinds of employment situations where many women are employed and do not have a strong bargaining position — day care centres, nursing homes, and retail outlets.

Unfortunately, despite its success in promoting meaningful negotiations and reducing conflict, opposition from business led the Manitoba Conservative government to repeal the FOS legislation in 1991. This, and the fanatical opposition of business to Ontario's modest legislation to "level the playing field" in industrial relations and guarantee the right of workers to organize and to collective bargaining, suggest that the struggle for legislative changes to facilitate organization of women workers will be a very difficult one. It is, however, an issue which should encourage a natural coalition between the women's movement and the labour movement.

Employment Standards and the Minimum Wage

Whether or not such changes in the climate for union organization are achieved, it will still be imperative to significantly upgrade federal and provincial employment standards. One reason is that, as Judy Fudge has pointed out in a 1992 article in *Canadian Dimension*, the "implicit and explicit state deregulation of the labour market" has led to a massive growth in non-standard work — part-time, short-term, own-account, and temporary-help agency work — which by 1987 comprised 33.8 per cent of all jobs. Whatever the union penetration of the labour force, these jobs are unlikely to be covered. Secondly, as long as there is unemployment and a "reserve army" of potential employees among housewives, the primary determinant of wages and other benefits in the secondary labour market will be legislated minimum wages and other employment standards. Thirdly, the existence of low wages and poor job security in the secondary labour market provides strong incentives for business to shift work from the primary labour market to the secondary labour market through sub-contracting and the replacement of traditional jobs with non-standard types of work. Fourthly, as we have shown, women are much less likely to be unionized than men.

Fudge argues that employment standards should be extended to include job security protection and measures to make it easier for women to balance domestic responsibilities with paid work including family and sick leave, a reduced work week and increased vacations. However, what is most immediately required is a substantial increase in minimum wages across the country to restore them in both real and relative terms to what they were two decades ago. In fact, minimum wage rate increases have fallen well behind inflation and behind average wage increases since the 1970s with the result that minimum wages in real terms have fallen by around 30 per cent and well below the 50 per cent of the average industrial wage that used to prevail. The National Council of Welfare's 1990 study, *Women and Poverty Revisited*, reported that average minimum wages across all jurisdictions in Canada fell from 49 per cent of average earnings in 1975 to 40 per cent by 1987. The people most affected by this relative decline are women since in 1986, two-thirds of all minimum-wage workers were women and most minimum-wage jobs were in female employment ghettos, retail trade, accommodation and food, and personal services. Gunderson, Muszynski and Keck, indeed, suggest that the appropriate policy to help combat female poverty among the working poor is to restore the minimum wage to a level of 50 per cent of the average industrial wage and maintain it at that level by indexation to the inflation rate.

Conclusion

Continued political pressure and education, improved legislation on a variety of fronts, and union action show some potential for lessening the economic inequality experienced by women in the workforce. The progress over the past decade, however slow and uneven, does indicate that these kinds of activity can have some impact. We would be wrong, however, to suggest that even with these means, any rapid or dramatic breakthrough is likely to occur. The sexual division of family work, social attitudes towards sexual inequality, and the supporting institutions are all deeply imbedded in the social fabric. Moreover, our market economy has become heavily dependent upon this inequality to provide the flexibility to adjust to the instabilities of the unplanned market economy. Furthermore, the direction of economic and technological change has been to increase inequality in the labour market while the continuing very high unemployment of the 1980s and into the '90s mitigates against pay and employment equity initiatives designed to combat this inequality. Given these factors, it is not even clear that the gains of the last decade or two can be retained.

If, as we have argued in Chapter 4, inequality is systemic, an intrinsic aspect of the functioning of our contemporary political economy, change will be required in the system itself, thereby running up against the inertia of social institutions and the opposition of all those with a vested interest in the status quo. The direction and pace of future change is far from clear.

Notes on Sources
and Further Reading

Ten years ago when we wrote the first edition of *Women and Work,* the first wave of secondary works on women's work had only recently become available, the result of the rise of the feminist movement and the growing public consciousness of women's issues. In the decade since the first edition, the interest in reclaiming women's role in history and advancing recognition of their contemporary economic and social contribution and of their equality rights has maintained the flow of academic, popular and government reports and studies. Indeed, the amount of new material has made the updating and revising of our analysis a considerably more onerous task than we initially envisioned. While progress toward equality has been slow, partial and subject to reversing forces, there have been some more substantial changes, perhaps most notably in the labour movement but also in pay and employment equity legislation and in education enrolment patterns. These changes we have tried to document and analyse in as comprehensive a manner as we could given this volume's limits of time and space.

We have again tried to consult as much of the primary and secondary material available, though we make no claim that our research has exhausted all, or even the majority, of the works and sources on the subject, particularly non-Canadian studies. We include here the major works consulted, both for the first and second edition, as a guide to those who wish to pursue some of the subject matter in greater depth, though some readers may also wish to check through the "Notes on Sources" in the first edition for some earlier titles that have perhaps been superseded by more recent work. The reader should be aware, however, that many other sources informed our research and writing, too many for all to be listed here. References are provided by topic rather than specifically by chapter, since some sources, particularly statistical sources, were used throughout the book.

Historical References

The material on women in the fur trade comes from Marjorie Wilkins Campbell's article, "Her Ladyship, My Squaw," published in *The Beaver*, September 1954, and from Sylvia Van Kirk's article, "The Impact of White Women on Fur Trade Society," found in *The Neglected Majority: Essays in Canadian Women's History*, edited by Susan Mann Trofimenkoff and Alison Prentice (Toronto: McClelland and Stewart, 1977). For a more detailed study, see Sylvia Van Kirk's *"Many Tender Ties": Women in Fur-Trade Society in Western Canada, 1670-1870* (Winnipeg: Watson and Dwyer, 1980).

Material on the work of pioneer women comes from *Pioneer and Gentlewomen of British America, 1713-1867*, edited by Beth Light and Alison Prentice (Toronto: New Hogtown Press, 1980). Comments on women in the fishing and craft industries are also based upon material found in this source, a very useful collection of documents. Additional information was taken from *A Harvest Yet to Reap: A History of Prairie Women*, by Linda Rasmussen *et al.* (Toronto: Women's Press, 1976). The quotation on page 11 is taken from this source.

Population figures were taken from J.S. Woodsworth's interesting book *My Neighbour: A Study of City Conditions. A Plea for Social Change*, first published by the Missionary Society of the Methodist Church in Toronto in 1911. Figures on the number of women in Montreal come from Suzanne Cross's "The Neglected Majority: The Changing Role of Women in Nineteenth Century Montreal," included in *The Neglected Majority*.

An indispensable source of material is a superb collection of articles under the title of *Women at Work*, edited by Janice Action, Penny Goldsmith and Bonnie Shepard (Toronto: Women's Press, 1974). Specific use was made of Genevieve Leslie's article "Domestic Service in Canada, 1880-1920" in reference to Eaton's advertising practices; Elizabeth Graham's article, "Schoolmarms and Early Teaching in Ontario," on teaching; Leo Johnson's article, "The Political Economy of Ontario Women in the Nineteenth Century," on industrial and economic activity; and Wayne Roberts and Alice Klein's "Besieged Innocence: The 'Problem' and Problems of Working Women — Toronto, 1896-1914." On the topic of teaching there is also Alison Prentice's article, "The Feminization of Teaching," found in *The Neglected Majority*, and the documentary collection edited by Alison Prentice and Susan Houston, *Family School and Society in Nineteenth Century Canada* (Toronto: Oxford University Press, 1974). For a discussion of overseas recruitment of domestic servants see Marilyn Barber's article, "The Women Ontario Welcomed: Immigrant Domestics for Ontario Homes, 1870-1930," in *The Neglected Majority: Essays in Canadian Women's History*, Vol. 2, pp. 102-121, edited by Alison Prentice and Susan Mann Trofimenkoff (Toronto: McClelland and Stewart, 1985). An invaluable complementary study to ours with our emphasis on paid work is Meg Luxton's *More than a Labour of Love: Three Generations of Women's Work in the Home* (Toronto: Women's Press, 1980).

There are several studies that analyse the social and living conditions of Ontario cities in the late nineteenth and early twentieth centuries, including *The People of Hamilton, Canada West: Family and Class in a Mid-Nineteenth-Century City* by Michael Katz (Cambridge, Mass.: Harvard University Press, 1975); *Hogtown: Working Class Toronto at the Turn of the Century* by Gregory Kealey (Toronto: New Hogtown Press, 1974); and Michael Piva's *The Condition of the Working Class in Toronto: 1900-1921* (Ottawa: University of Ottawa Press, 1979). Wayne Roberts addresses conditions for women in his book, *Honest Womanhood: Feminism, Femininity and Class Consciousness Among Toronto Working Women 1893-1914* (Toronto: New Hogtown Press, 1976).

On Montreal there is the famous study by Herbert Brown Ames, frequently referred to in the text, *The City Below the Hill: A Sociological Study of a Portion of the City of Montreal, Canada*, originally published in Montreal by Bishop Engraving and Printing in 1897 and reprinted by the University of Toronto Press in 1972. Terry Copp has used Ames's material plus much additional material in his book, *The Anatomy of Poverty: The Condition of the Working Class in Montreal, 1897-1929* (Toronto: McClelland and Stewart, 1974).

There are a number of excellent articles dealing with women in industrializing Montreal. Perhaps the most useful work is that of Bettina Bradbury, including "The Family Economy and Work in an Industrializing City, Montreal, 1871," *Historical Papers* (1979):71-96; "The Fragmented Family: Family Strategies in the Face of Death, Illness and Poverty, Montreal, 1860-1885," in *Childhood and Family in Canadian History*, pp. 109-128, edited by Joy Parr (Toronto: McClelland and Stewart, 1982); and "Women and Wage Labour in a Period of Transition: Montreal, 1861-1881," *Histoire Social-So-*

cial History, volume 17, May 1984, which was very useful in preparing this section. Also useful was Marta Danylewycz's paper to the Canadian Historical Association in 1980, "Through Women's Eyes: The Family in Late Nineteenth Century Quebec." An article that looks at the textile industry in Quebec in the slightly later period is Gail Cuthbert Brandt's "Weaving It Together: Life Cycle and the Industrial Experience of Female Cotton Workers in Quebec, 1910-1950," published in *Labour/Le Travailleur*, Spring 1981. On industrial home sewing in Canada from the late nineteenth century to the present, see Laura C. Johnson with Robert E. Johnson, *The Seam Allowance* (Toronto: Women's Press, 1982). The material on the Ganong Brothers confectionery is from a fascinating study by Margaret McCallum, "Separate Spheres: the Organization of Work in a Confectionery Factory: Ganong Bros., St. Stephen, New Brunswick," published in *Labour/Le Travail*, 24 (Fall) 1989, though we may disagree with her conclusion based on our different conception of the meaning of a "reserve army" in a segmented labour market.

Of further interest are Gail Cuthbert Brandt's article, "The Transformation of Women's Work in the Quebec Cotton Industry, 1920-1950," in *The Character of Class Struggle: Essays in Canadian Working-Class History, 1850-1985*, pp. 115-137, edited by Bryan D. Palmer (Toronto: McClelland and Stewart, 1986) and Mercedes Steedman's article, "Skill and Gender in the Canadian Clothing Industry, 1890-1940," in *On the Job: Confronting the Labour Process in Canada*, pp. 152-176, edited by Craig Heron and Robert Storey (Montreal: McGill-Queens University Press, 1986).

Material on rural life can be found in John MacDougall's *Rural Life in Canada: Its Trend and Tasks*, first published in 1913 and reprinted by the University of Toronto Press in 1973. For material on the development of the Canadian dairy industry see Marjorie Griffin Cohen's interesting article, "The Decline of Women in Canadian Dairying" in *The Neglected Majority: Essays in Canadian Women's History*, Vol. 2, pp. 61-83, edited by Alison Prentice and Susan Mann Trofimenkoff (Toronto: McClelland and Stewart, 1985).

The impact of the industrial and organizational revolution in Central Canada is analysed in Gregory Kealey's 1980 study, *Toronto Workers Respond to Industrial Capitalism 1867-1892* (Toronto: University of Toronto Press). A somewhat similar study of Hamilton is Bryan Palmer's *A Culture of Conflict* (Montreal: McGill-Queen's University Press, 1979). Kealey is also editor of the 1973 University of Toronto Press reprint of the 1889 Royal Commission on the Relations of Labour and Capital, published under the title *Canada Investigates Industrialism*. This is an invaluable contemporary account of hours, working conditions and wages to which we have made frequent reference. Other royal commissions whose evidence is important are the *Royal Commission to Investigate Industrial Disputes in the Cotton Factories of the Province of Quebec*, 1908; and the *Royal Commission Regarding the Dispute Regarding Hours of Employment Between the Bell Telephone Company of Canada Ltd. and Operators at Toronto, Ontario*, 1907.

For detailed studies of the impact of industrialization on women see Joy Parr's book, *The Gender of Breadwinners: Women, Men, and Change in Two Industrial Towns: 1880-1950* (Toronto: University of Toronto Press, 1990) and Marjorie Griffin Cohen's book, *Women's Work, Markets, and Economic Development in Nineteenth-Century Ontario* (Toronto: University of Toronto Press, 1988). Specific information on the involvement of women in factories in 1871 taken from the 1871 Census can be found in Elizabeth Bloomfield and G.T. Bloomfield, *Canadian Women in Workshops, Mills and Factories*, (Guelph: University of Guelph Press, 1991).

Another important source of contemporary material is Irving Abella and David Millar's edited collection *The Canadian Worker in the Twentieth Century* (Toronto: Oxford University Press, 1978), which includes the "Videre" articles written in 1912 for *The Toronto Star* and excerpts from the memoirs of Jean McDonald, covering 1877-1969. There is also *Women of Canada: Their Life and Work*, published by the National Council of Women in Canada in 1900 and reprinted in 1975. On women with university educations, there is Veronica Strong-Boag's article "Canada's Women Doctors: Feminism Constrained," in *A Not Unreasonable Claim: Women and Social Reform in Canada*, edited by Linda Kealey (Toronto: Women's Press, 1979). Work on the organizational revolution in white-collar work as a result of the growth of big business during this century has been done by Graham S. Lowe. It is summed up in "The Administrative Revolution in the Canadian Office: An Overview," in *Work in the Canadian Context*, edited by Katherina L.P. Lundy and Barbara D. Warme (Toronto: Butterworths, 1981, 2nd ed. 1986). See also his discussion of this subject in "Mechanization, Feminization, and Managerial Control in the Early Twentieth-Century Canadian Office," in *On the Job: Confronting the Labour*

Process in Canada, pp. 177-209, edited by Craig Heron and Robert Storey (Montreal: McGill-Queen's University Press, 1986) and *Women in the Administrative Revolution: The Feminization of Clerical Work* (Toronto: University of Toronto Press, 1987).

For the period of the First World War, see Ceta Ramkhalawansingh's article "Women During the Great War," published in *Women at Work*. There are also several primary sources, including two by Marjory MacMurchy, *The Woman—God Bless Her* (Toronto: S.B. Grundy, 1916), and *The Canadian Girl at Work* (Toronto: A.T. Wilgress, 1919). The classic in the area from which the majority of analysis is drawn is Enid (Price) Bone's *Changes in the Industrial Occupations of Women in the Environment of Montreal During the Period of the War, 1914-1918* (Montreal: McGill University Press, 1919).

Useful sources for the later periods include A. Oddson's report for the Economic Survey Board in 1939, *Employment of Women in Manitoba*, and the edited collection by Michiel Horn, *The Dirty Thirties: Canadians in the Great Depression* (Toronto: Copp Clark, 1972). This latter is an excellent collection of material from, and dealing with, the thirties. See also Veronica Strong-Boag's treatment of the inter-war period, *The New Day Recalled: Lives of Girls and Women in English Canada, 1919-1939* (Toronto: Copp Clark Pitman Ltd., 1988). The discussion of the ideological conception of the proper role of women in the labour market demonstrated in the debate over unemployment insurance is taken from Ruth Roach Pierson, "Gender and the Unemployment Insurance Debates in Canada, 1934-1940," *Labour/Le Travail*, volume 25 (Spring) 1990.

For a concise description of the movement of women into the work force during the Second World War see Ruth Pierson's article "Women's Emancipation and the Recruitment of Women into the Canadian Labour Force in W.W.II," found in *The Neglected Majority*. See also her works, *Canadian Women and the Second World War* (Ottawa: the Canadian Historical Association, 1983) and *"They're Still Women After All": The Second World War and Canadian Womanhood* (Toronto: McClelland and Stewart, 1986).

For statistical sources additional to those mentioned above and the decennial *Census*, we have made frequent recourse to M.C. Urquhart and K.A.H. Buckley's encyclopaedic and invaluable *Historical Statistics of Canada* (Toronto: Macmillan, 1965). We also consulted David Millar's regrettably unpublished data on real wages in Canada over the last century.

Women's Participation and Wages

The sources used for Chapters 2 and 3 are primarily of two types, statistical data drawn from official government sources, and secondary analyses, frequently by government agencies or in the form of labour economics monographs or texts, based on official statistical sources. The primary statistical sources for labour market data are the *Census* (quinquennial and decennial) and Statistics Canada, *The Labour Force* (monthly) and *The Labour Force: Annual Averages* (annual since 1990). The latter includes all the basic data on employment and unemployment by age, sex, occupation, industry, full- and part-time employees, personal and family responsibilities and province. Special surveys, including annual work patterns, absence from work, child care arrangements, work histories and a host of other specific aspects of labour market behaviour which used to be published in *The Labour Force*, are now published in a separate quarterly publication, *Perspectives*. The major source of income data was Statistics Canada, *Earnings of Men and Women* and the Department of Labour compendium, *Women in the Labour Force*. Unfortunately, the latest edition of *Women in the Labour Force* provides data only up to 1987 and in some cases it is difficult to reconcile the figures in it with other statistical sources.

Earlier labour market statistics are taken from secondary sources and analyses, including: *Opportunity for Choice*, edited by Gail C.A. Cook for Statistics Canada in association with the C.D. Howe Research Institute published in 1976 (see, in particular "Family: Functions, Formation, and Fertility" by Monica Boyd, Margrit Eichler and John R. Hofley from which we quote, and "Work Patterns" by Morley Gunderson from which we have taken some important data and analysis); *Labour Economics in Canada*, by Sylvia Ostry and Mahmood A. Zaidi, published in 1979; and "Labour Markets and Sex Differences in Canadian Incomes" prepared by Monica Boyd and Elizabeth Humphreys for the Economic Council of Canada in 1979. Some statistics for the earlier edition and included here were taken from a statistical compendium compiled by the Manitoba Department of Labour in 1981, *Women in the Manitoba Labour Market*.

More recent sources of statistical analysis include: Ontario Government, *Green Paper on Pay Equity*, Toronto, 1985; Jac-Andre Boulet and Laval Lavalee, *The Changing Economic Status of Women*, Economic Council of Canada, 1984; Pat Connelly and

Martha MacDonald, *Women and the Labour Force*, Statistics Canada, 1990; John Myles, G. Picot, and T. Wannell, *Wages and Jobs in the 1980s: Changing Youth Wages and the Declining Middle*, published by Statistics Canada in 1988, and a subsequent 1991 study by the same authors, *Good Jobs, Bad Jobs and the Declining Middle*; the National Council of Welfare's *Women and Poverty Revisited and Pension Reform*, both published in 1990; and perhaps the most useful single source, *Women and Labour Market Poverty*, by Morley Gunderson, Leon Muszynski, and Jennifer Keck, written for the Canadian Advisory Council on the Status of Women in 1990. This contains a wealth of information, analysis and policy recommendations relevant to a number of chapters in our work. In fact, all these studies are relied on for the background information underlying the analysis and recommendations in Chapters 4, 5 and 7. The cost of raising children was taken from the Manitoba Department of Agriculture's handbook, *Family Resource Management Guide*, 1991. This updates the estimate in Wayne Lilley's article, "The Bottom Line on Baby," in the *Financial Post Magazine*, April 1981.

Particular information on education comes from three Statistics Canada publications, *Teachers in Universities, Universities Enrollment and Degrees*, and *Community Colleges and Related Institutions: Postsecondary Enrollment and Degrees*.

One of the more useful earlier studies of housework in Canada by Susan Clark and Marylee Stephenson, "Housework as Real Work," is included in the collection edited by Katherine Lundy and Barbara Warme, *Work in the Canadian Context* (Toronto: Butterworths, 1981). The work of Meg Luxton is also important; see, for instance, "Taking on the Double Day: Housewives as a Reserve Army of Labour," *Atlantis* 7,1 (1981). However the best and most readable, recent comprehensive survey is *Few Choices: Women, Work and Family*, by Ann Duffy, Nancy Mandell and Norene Pupo, published by Garamond in its Network Basics Series in 1989. Of course, the classic study of the double burden of house and market work, now out in a second edition, is Pat and Hugh Armstrong's *The Double Ghetto* (Toronto: McClelland and Stewart, 1984, first published 1978).

Segmented Labour Markets

The amount of material on segmented labour markets and the application of segmented labour market theory to the problems of women in the labour market was already large when we wrote the first edition of this book. In the decade since it has increased substantially (although strangely, it has not found its way into orthodox labour economics texts which usually fail to deal with systemic discrimination in a realistic way). The pioneering work in segmented labour market theory was *Internal Labor Markets and Manpower Analysis* by P.B. Doeringer and M.J. Piore (Lexington, Mass.: D.C. Heath, 1971) which has since come out in a second edition. Piore has also written a number of subsequent articles and books and edited several collections on the subject, including *Dualism and Discontinuity in Industrial Societies* (with Suzanne Berger, Cambridge: Cambridge University Press, 1984) and *Unemployment and Inflation* (White Plains: Sharpe, 1979). A somewhat different slant to the general theme is given by Edna Bonacich in "The Past, Present, and Future of Split Labor Market Theory," *Research in Race and Ethnic Relations*, 1979. Perhaps the best survey integrating the historical evolution of the labour process with dual labour market theory in the American context is Richard Edwards, *Contested Terrain*, (New York: Basic Books, 1979). A much more modest attempt in the Canadian context is Paul Phillips, *Canadian Political Economy* (Toronto: Garamond, 1990).

There has not been a great deal of theoretical or empirical work in the formal area of segmented labour market economics in Canada outside of some studies for the Economic Council of Canada and Statistics Canada, though there is a burgeoning labour process literature which also relates to labour market segmentation. Two of the best recent collections that are well worth reading are Craig Heron and Robert Storey, eds., *On the Job* (Montreal: McGill-Queens University Press, 1986) and Graham Lowe and Harvey Krahn, eds., *Working Canadians* (Toronto: Methuen, 1984). Some of the most interesting work on women and work in the Maritimes, in particular in relation to the fishing industry, is included in a number of articles by Joan McFarland and by Pat Connelly and Martha MacDonald. Two worth mentioning in particular are McFarland's "Changing Modes of Social Control in a New Brunswick Fish Packing Town," *Studies in Political Economy*, 4 (Autumn) 1980, and Connelly and MacDonald's "Women's Work: Domestic and Wage Labour in a Nova Scotia Community," *Studies in Political Economy* 10 (Winter) 1983.

Earlier, more labour market oriented studies include: Harish Jain, "Employment and Pay Discrimination in Canada: Theories, Evidence, and Policies," in *Union-Management Relations in Canada*, edited by John Anderson and Morley Gunderson (Don Mills: Addison-Wesley, 1982); Chan F. Aw, "A Dual Labour Market Analyis: A Study of Canadian Manufacturing Industries," a discussion paper for Labour Canada, 1980; Paul Phillips, ed., *Manpower Issues in Manitoba*, Manitoba Economic Development Advisory Board, 1975; and Christine Rollo, "An Investigation of Variables Affecting Male/Female Wage Differentials in the Retail Food Industry in Winnipeg," unpublished M.A. thesis, University of Manitoba, 1980. For an explicitly Marxist analysis of the female labour market in Canada see Pat Connelly, *Last Hired, First Fired* (Toronto: Women's Press, 1978).

Technology, Free Trade and Economic Restructuring

The advent of the new microelectronic and related technologies has excited the imagination of large numbers of writers and prognosticators, both those that can be labelled optimists and those that can be considered pessimists about the impact of the new technologies on the world of work. Perhaps the best recent comprehensive survey is Heather Menzies' *Fast Forward and Out of Control* (Toronto: McClelland and Stewart, 1989) which updates and significantly broadens the analysis of her seminal study *Women and the Chip: Case Studies of the Effects of Informatics on Employment in Canada* (Montreal: Institute for Research on Public Policy, 1980). Earlier background information came from "Special Report," *Business Week*, 3 August 1981; "At the Centre: The Chips are Down, " *Canadian Dimension*, December 1981; and "The New Electronic Canada" by Marc Belanger, *The Facts* (CUPE) 5,7 (September) 1983.

The specific effects of microelectronic technology on retail trade are explored in Julie White's *Trouble in Store? The Impact of Microelectronics in the Retail Trade* prepared for the Women's Bureau of Labour Canada, 1985. A very readable and accessible Canadian discussion of the new technology and clerical workers is contained in Marcy Cohen and Margaret White, *Taking Control of Our Future: Clerical Workers and the New Technology* (Vancouver: Women's Skill Development Society, 1987). American sources are numerous. Three that were consulted are: Heidi Hartman, Robert Kraut and Louise Tilley, eds., *Computer Chips and Paper Clips*, vols. 1 and 2 (Washington: National Research Council-National Academy Press, 1986 and 1987), and Robert Kraut, *Technology and the Transformation of White-Collar Work* (Hillsdale, NJ.: Lawrence Erlbaum Association, 1987). On the impact of VDT technology on women's health see Julianne Polle, "A Multivariate Analysis of the Non-Radiation Health Effects of Video Display Terminals," unpublished MA Thesis, University of Manitoba, 1984.

The seminal work on the impact of free trade on women is the 1987 study by Marjorie Cohen, *Free Trade and the Future of Women's Work* (Toronto: Garamond and the Canadian Centre for Policy Alternatives, Network Basics Series).

Women and Unions

Resource material on women and unions can be divided into three categories: historical accounts, contemporary analyses and documentary material (for example, collective agreement surveys), and statistical sources. In the first edition, we relied heavily on Julie White's *Women and Unions*, (Ottawa: Canadian Advisory Council on the Status of Women, 1980) for information in all these areas. In this edition we have updated much of this material, which is a not inconsequential task given the significant progress of women within labour's agenda and organization over the last decade. Perhaps one of the best examples of this is the study, again by Julie White, *Mail and Female: Women and the Canadian Union of Postal Workers* (Toronto: Thompson Educational Publishers, 1990).

More specifically on the history of women's participation in unionism, we utilized many of the same sources as were consulted in the chapter on the history of women's work. The majority of the material on the early unionization of women comes from Wayne Roberts's excellent book *Honest Womanhood* and the article he wrote with Alice Klein, "Beseiged Innocence," in *Women at Work*. Union material is also included in the reports of the *Royal Commission on the Relations of Labour and Capital* (1889), the *Commission to Investigate Whether, and If So, to What Extent, the Sweating System is Practised in the Various Centres of the Dominion* (1896), and the 1908 *Royal Commission to Investigate Industrial Disputes in the Cotton Factories of the Province of Quebec*.

Sexism in the early labour movement comes up in a number of places. For a general view of the U.S. and British experience, see the review article by Dorothy E. Smith, "Women and Trade Unions," in *Resources for Feminist Research*, July 1981. References to the attitudes of men to women in Canada can be found in Roberts and in White, who also outlines how the government consulted middle-class women when writing up protective legislation for working-class women. For a detailed descussion of how this worked in British Columbia, there is Marie Campbell's informative article "Sexism in British Columbia Trade Unions, 1900-1920," published in *In Her Own Right: Selected Essays on Women's History in B.C.*, edited by Barbara Latham and Cathy Kerr (Victoria: Camosun College, 1980). Campbell and White also discuss how unions would negotiate for lower wages for women. Campbell includes a discussion of the role of men in the 1906 telephone operators' strike in Vancouver. On the history of women and the B.C. Telephone Company see Elaine Bernard's excellent study, *The Long Distance Feeling*, (Vancouver: New Star, 1982). Note that her account of the 1906 strike differs somewhat from Campbell in the matter of the support from the male linemen. See also Bernard's account of the 1919 operators' strike in "Last Back: Folklore and the Telephone Operators in the 1919 Vancouver General Strike," *Not Just Pin Money*, edited by Barbara Latham and Roberta Pazdro, (Victoria: Camosun College, 1984). For a treatment of the strike of Bell Telephone operators in Toronto in 1907, see Joan Sangster's article, "The 1907 Bell Telephone Strike: Organizing Women Workers," in *Labour/Le Travailleur*, volume 3, 1978. This is a useful discussion of the strike, which resulted in the *Royal Commission Regarding the Dispute Regarding Hours of Employment Between the Bell Telephone Company of Canada Ltd. and Operators at Toronto, Ontario*, 1907.

For a discussion of what effect the First World War had on unionization, see White and Campbell's work already cited and Ceta Ramkhalawansingh's article "Women During the Great War" in *Women and Work*. Other sources consulted on this period and earlier include Shirley Tillotson, "We may all soon be 'first-class men': Gender and skill in Canada's early twentieth century urban telegraph industry," *Labour/Le Travail*, Volume 27 (Spring) 1991; Bob Russell, "A Fair or a Minimum Wage? Women Workers, the State, and the Origins of Wage Regulation in Western Canada," *Labour/Le Travail*, volume 28 (Fall) 1991; Jacques Ferland, "In Search of the Unbound Prometheia," *Labour/Le Travail*, volume 24 (Fall) 1989;

and Ruth Frager, "Sewing Solidarity: The Eaton's Strike of 1912," *Canadian Woman Studies*, Volume 7 (3).

Material on the 1924-27 movement of the Amalgamated Clothing Workers is taken from Terry Copp, *The Anatomy of Poverty*. Gail Cuthbert Brandt describes the Federation of Textile Workers in "Weaving it Together: Life Cycle and the Industrial Experience of Female Cotton Workers in Quebec, 1910-1950," *Labour/Le Travailleur*, Volume 7, 1981. A discussion of the 1931 strike of the International Ladies Garment Workers Union is available in Catherine Macleod, "Women in Production: The Toronto Dressmakers' Strike of 1931," in *Women at Work*. The 1934 strike is discussed in Evelyn Dumas' well-known article "The Shmatta Strikes," published in *The Bitter Thirties in Quebec* (Montreal: Black Rose Books, 1975). Sara Diamond's quote about women's auxiliaries is from "A Union Man's Wife: The Ladies' Auxiliary Movement in the IWA, The Lake Cowichan Experience," in Latham and Pazdro, eds., *Not Just Pin Money*.

On Eaton's in the thirties there is the article "Working for Eaton's, 1934" found in Michiel Horn's collection *The Dirty Thirties: Canadians in the Great Depression*. More recent is Eileen (Tallman) Sufrin, *The Eaton Drive* (Toronto: Fitzhenry and Whiteside, 1982). There are few secondary sources on the 1984-85 Eaton's strikes. The one exception we found is Errol Black's "The Struggle Against Eaton's Moves to Manitoba," *Canadian Dimension*, March 1986. Other sources used were various issues of several daily newspapers, *McLean's*, the Ontario Federation of Labour's *Ontario Labour*, and the CLC's *Canadian Labour*.

For information on the effect of the Second World War on the unionization of women, see Desmond Morton and Terry Copp, *Working People: An Illustrated History of Canadian Labour* (Ottawa: Deneau and Greenberg, 1980) and other general histories of the Canadian labour movement, in particular H.A. Logan, *Trade Unions in Canada: Their Development and Functioning* (Toronto: Macmillan, 1948), and Charles Lipton, *The Trade Union Movement of Canada, 1827-1959* (Montreal: Canadian Social Publications, 1966). These sources also deal with the postwar union developments, including the 1946 textile workers' strike. Also to be consulted on that strike is "Madeleine Parent: Valleyfield's Textile Workers, 1946" in Gloria Montero's *We Stood Together* (Toronto: James Lorimer, 1979). Lipton also deals with the 1952 Dominion Textile strike. The evolution of the Postal Worker's Union in its attitudes and sensitivity to women is recounted in Julie White, *Mail and Female*. A detailed discussion on the problems of organizing bank workers in the last decade can be found in Rosemary Warskett, "Bank Worker Unionization and the Law," *Studies in Political Economy* 25(1988).

Contemporary data on women in unions come from three major sources, Part 2 of Statistics Canada's annual publication *Corporations and Labour Unions Returns Act* (better known as CALURA), which reports on labour union membership including male and female distribution; Statistics Canada, *Women and the Labour Market*; and a series of papers published by the Industrial Relations Centre, Queen's University. The three utilized here are Pradeep Kumar and David Cowan, *Gender Differences in Union Membership Status: The Role of Labour Market Segmentation*, (1989); Pradeep Kumar, *Union Beliefs and Attitudes of Canadian Workers: An Econometric Analysis*, (1991); and Pradeep Kumar and Lynn Acri, *Women's Issues and Collective Bargaining*, (1991) which gives extensive data on women's issues in collective bargaining. Labour Canada's *Directory of Labour Organization* has extensive union statistics and in some aspects is more complete than CALURA. Unfortunately, however, it does not report on the gender distribution of membership.

Though a little dated now, *Union Sisters: Women in the Labour Market*, edited by Linda Briskin and Lynda Yanz (Toronto, Women's Educational Press, 1983) deals in much greater detail with most of the issues discussed here. Fortunately, on the matter of women in union leadership and labour's agenda, Linda Briskin has added a more recent assessment in her article "Women, Unions and Leadership" in *Canadian Dimension*, 24, 1 (January-February) 1990. On the relation between union strategy and labour and employment standards, see Judy Fudge, "Solidarity Strategies for a Polarized Labour Market," *Canadian Dimension*, 26, 1 (January-February) 1992. The general discussion on the impact of unions on wages and benefits is taken from two sources, Morley Gunderson and Craig Riddell's Canadian textbook, *Labour Market Economics* (Toronto: McGraw-Hill Ryerson, 1988); and from an American study by Richard Freeman and James Medoff (for which there is no comparable Canadian source), *What Do Unions Do?* (New York: Basic Books, 1984). Peter Warrian's quotation regarding union representatives is from a paper, "Patriarchy and Trade Unions," presented to the Society of Socialist Studies in Ottawa in 1982. The neo-Conservative assault on unions and collective bargaining, with the consequent negative implications for women, is documented in Leo Panitch and Donald Swartz, *The Assault on Trade Union Freedoms: From Consent to Coercion Revisited* (Toronto: Garamond, 1988).

Proposals for Change

Our discussion of the potential policy alternatives to deal with gender inequality in the labour market in the first edition was based on Gail C.A. Cook and Mary Eberts, "Policies Affecting Work," in *Opportunity for Choice*, and the specific legislative measures listed in the reports of the Royal Commission on the Status of Women and the *Ten Years Later* update by the Advisory Council on the Status of Women. Since then, much has happened, perhaps most importantly the spread of pay and employment equity plans at the governmental level. An excellent survey and analysis of the state of pay equity is Judy Fudge and Patricia McDermott, eds., *Just Wages* (Toronto: University of Toronto Press, 1991). Particularly useful were the editors' "Conclusion," Pat and Hugh Armstrong's "Limited Possibilities and Possible Limits for Pay Equity," and Isabella Bakker's "Pay Equity and Economic Restructuring: The Polarization of Policy?" though all of the contributions are worth reading. On employment equity there is no such general assessment. However, the Canadian Human Rights Commission background paper, "The Canadian Human Rights Commission and Employment Equity, 1987-1991" published in January 1992, is a good place to start. Annual updates on legislation and programs are usually included in the Queen's University Industrial Relations Centre's "Industrial Relations: Trends and Emerging Issues." Professor Leo-Paul Lauzon's survey of female senior executives and directors is reported in an article by Barrie McKenna, "Women face closed door to boardrooms" in the *Globe and Mail*, June 30, 1992. We have already referred the reader to the reports of the National Council of Welfare and to Gunderson, Muszynski and Keck's excellent *Women and Labour Market Poverty*, which come to policy conclusions that are, for the most part, very similar to ours.

This is certainly not, in any sense, a complete bibliography. It is meant to be a guide of the most important sources used in this current edition and contains all those that we quote directly or indirectly. A complete bibliography would be a book in itself. Indeed, there are several such bibliographies that readers interested in a specific topic might wish to explore. A few specific Canadian bibliographies include: Evelyn Bayefsky, *Women and the Status of Part-time Work: A Review and Annotated Bibliography* (Toronto: Ontario Library Review, 1977); Sara Diamond, *Women's Labour History in British Columbia: A Bibliography, 1930-1948* (Vancouver: Press Gang, 1980); *Employment Equity: An Annotated Bibliography* (Toronto: Ontario Women's Directorate, 1990); John Ford and Alan Miller, *Women, Microelectronics, and Employment: A Selected Bibliography* (Toronto: Ontario Ministry of Labour Library, 1983); and Carol Mazur and Sheila Pepper, *Women and Canada: A Bibliography, 1965-82* (Toronto: McMaster University Library, 1984). In addition, useful bibliographies can be found at the end of many of the secondary sources listed here, in particular the one included in Gunderson, Muszynski and Keck.

Index